## ADVANCE PRA[

Dr. Ward does an excellent job of leveraging careful exegesis about an historically misunderstood book to help Christian readers understand its truly theological assumptions and implications. His summary of the canonical intertextuality of Esther is compelling for those who wish to live a "biblical" life in a Pagan World.

**Timothy S. Laniak**
Dean and Professor of Old Testament
Gordon-Conwell Theological Seminary
Author of *Esther* (Understanding the Bible Commentary)

For many, the book of Esther remains one of the strangest works in the Old Testament. What are we to make of a book which never mentions God and whose central characters all seem flawed in key ways? Is it even possible to read this text theologically? In a clear and informed way, Nathan Ward tackles these issues head on. Placing his approach in the wider history of interpretation, he shows how the book works theologically through its interaction with the rest of the canon. From this, he shows how it continues to provide guidance for Christian readers today. This helpful study enables Christians to understand why we need this strange book in our canon.

**David G. Firth**
Lecturer in Old Testament
St. Johns College, Nottingham
Author of *The Message of Esther* (The Bible Speaks Today)

Nathan Ward has produced a well-informed study of Esther, which examines fairly the many complexities of the book, offers intriguing intra-textual connections with other Scriptures, and suggests some helpful spiritual lessons which can be derived from its text. *God Unseen* should appeal to teachers, pastors, and students of Scripture.

**Edwin M. Yamauchi**
Professor of History Emeritus
Miami University
Author of *Persia and the Bible*

*God Unseen* combines accessibility with new thought-provoking insights. ... [I]t is a compelling read not least for Christian disciples who look to the biblical text for inspiration while living in a world which often is oblivious to the presence of the unseen God. I thoroughly enjoyed reading this book and recommend it to others—it is grounded in scholarship and rooted in the personal, thoughtful faith of its author.

**Debra Reid**
**Spurgeon's College, London**
**Author of *Esther* (Tyndale Old Testament Commentaries)**

In this work Ward offers an incisive and instructive look into Esther through historical, exegetical, and practical lenses. Through thoughtful and penetrating analysis, Ward offers a fresh approach to the study of the book of Esther that is sure to benefit scholars and pastors alike.

**Scott Manor**
**Vice President of Academic Affairs, Dean of Faculty**
**Knox Theological Seminary**

The story of Esther creates several interesting problems from a biblical-theological and canonical perspective, especially for Protestants who regard the Hebrew text alone as Christian Scripture. Sadly, this often goes unrecognized in the Church. In Nathan Ward's *God Unseen*, readers will find a helpful introduction that is sensitive to the difficulties of Esther as well as a compelling articulation of a nuanced traditional reading of this fascinating narrative.

**John Anthony Dunne**
**Author of *Esther and Her Elusive God***

This book is an excellent starting point for the reader who wants a better understanding of the Book of Esther. It provides a helpful survey of what earlier interpreters have said about the book and its puzzling features. In contrast to several modern scholars, Ward argues that the Book of Esther contains a religious message, despite the apparent "absence" of God in it. By a careful study of references to other Biblical texts ("interbiblical dialogue"), the use of different literary techniques, the remarkable apparent "coincidences" in the text, and especially the dramatic reversals at the center of the book, Ward makes a strong case for the theological nature of the Book of Esther. From there he seeks to demonstrate the relevance of the Book of Esther for issues confronting the contemporary Church. *God Unseen* provides a balanced diet of information, exposition, and application of the text.

**Max F. Rogland**
**Associate Professor of Old Testament and Associate Dean**
**Erskine Theological Seminary**
**Author of *Esther* (Zondervan Exegetical Commentary on the Old Testament, forthcoming)**

Ward's book on Esther is a very useful book for Christians who want to take up the challenge of reading and understanding an often neglected, misunderstood, and under-valued book in the Old Testament. Ward not only discusses helpful introductory material about the book of Esther's literary genre, historicity, and canonicity, but also explores the critical question of how Christians living in a world that some days looks a lot like the unpredictable and godless world of ancient Persia can find the unseen God in the book that does not mention God, the land, the covenant, prayer or God's law. Pastors and students will find this very readable book very helpful resource.

**Marion Taylor**
**Professor of Old Testament**
**Wycliffe College at the University of Toronto**
**Author of *Esther* (Story of God Bible Commentary, forthcoming)**

# God Unseen

## A Theological Introduction to Esther

Nathan Ward

*God Unseen: An Introduction to the Book of Esther*
© 2016 by DeWard Publishing Company, Ltd.
P.O. Box 6259, Chillicothe, Ohio 45601
800.300.9778
**www.deward.com**

Cover design by Barry Wallace.

Printed in the United States of America.

ISBN: 978-1-936341-80-1

*To Brooke*

# Contents

# *Preface*

Several years ago, I began a thorough study of Esther because I believed that no one had done much with it before. While this was a natural expectation, given the amount of time it receives in most churches across America, it turns out to be woefully incorrect in terms of scholarship. By the time I learned how frequently Esther is written about, it was too late: I had joined the rank of Esther students who wanted nothing more than to exhaust every corner of study in the book. So I continued.

My studies led to teaching classes on Esther in congregational and collegiate settings as well as giving a series of Esther lectures at the Florida College Annual Lectureship over a few years' period of time. A few years later, I began a Doctor of Ministry program in Theological Exegesis. As my coursework continued and my Esther reading, while slowed, marched on, I quickly became convinced that I would turn my study in Esther into my Major Project. The book in your hands is a modification of that work.

There are many to whom I owe a debt of gratitude for the ability to complete this book—first, two scholars who were willing to converse about various matters related to the study: Dr. David deSilva, who was willing to look at an early draft of the proposal of my major project, offering helpful suggestions, and then to discuss further the Septuagint additions in Esther, which helped make the first chapter of this book stronger overall; and Dr. John Anthony Dunne for his willingness to chat with a complete stranger about the book of Esther on Facebook, which helped clarify some of his positions and gave me a sounding board to think further through mine.

Three people deserve particular recognition for helping clean up this manuscript: first, Dr. Orrey McFarland for his help as thesis supervisor of my major project, providing excellent criticism and valuable advice along the way; next, Dene Ward, my mom, proofed each chapter's rough draft before it went any further, cleaning up the writing and catching mistakes that should have been obvious to me in my first edit; finally, the book version received a final proofing and edit by Mrs. Loretta Atherton. My relationship with Loretta has been long and varied: first, I knew her as the mother of a summer camp friend; next, I knew her as a demanding freshman composition teacher; now, she is a professional colleague at Florida College, where we both labor to help shape students into critical thinking adults.

Most significantly, thanks must go to my wife, Brooke, who has supported me through my education and has had many evenings alone with our young sons while I hammered away at the keyboard or the books. Her support has been invaluable, and I do not doubt for a minute that I could not have completed the coursework or this book without her by my side. As I dedicated my major project, so it is to her that I dedicate this work.

# PART ONE

---

# The Interpretation of Esther

# ONE

# *A History of Interpretation*

The interpretation of Esther has taken various forms, whether the additions made to the text in its translations or the additions made in the interpretive process, from the midrashic flourishes of Rabbis to the moralizing of the medieval Christians. A common question that seems to run through these writings is whether there is any religious value to Esther. Since it seems to be such a secular story—no explicit mention of God, the promises, the temple, the Law, etc.—there has always been debate about how to interpret the story and its characters. In this part of the book, I will trace the history of the interpretation of Esther and then examine two key issues related to the history of interpretation: first, the question of canonicity, which is directly tied to the religious question; second, the issue of historicity and genre, which has become a primary focus in Esther studies over the last several decades. These issues will be examined to show the question of religion in Esther has continually been a subject of concern, which will set the stage for part 2 and its argument for the religious nature of the book of Esther as a whole.

## A. Greek Versions

The textual situation of the book of Esther is, to say the least, complex. In addition to the Masoretic Text (MT), there are two different Greek versions. Neither of the Greek versions is a straightforward translation of the MT, and while there are significant similarities between them (e.g., they share six additions), there are also important differences (e.g., what is called the Alpha Text [AT] is roughly 20% shorter than the Septuagint [LXX]).[1] Scholars debate whether the AT represents an independent Hebrew textual tradition (known as the proto-AT) or if it is merely a further development of the LXX. Furthermore, there is debate whether the MT removed religious language[2] or if the Greek versions added it.[3]

While it may not appear directly relevant, the principles of textual criticism may apply here. In particular, three of the principles of internal criticism seem to be helpful in sorting through the various versions of Esther.[4] First, the critic is to prefer the shorter reading, since scribes tended to add to rather than shorten the text. Second, the critic is to prefer the more difficult reading, since scribes tended to remove difficulties rather than create them. Finally, the critic is to prefer the reading that best explains

---

[1] See John Anthony Dunne, *Esther and Her Elusive God: How a Secular Story Functions as Scripture* (Euguene: Wipf and Stock, 2014), 131–136 for a helpful summary of the issues surrounding LXX and AT. Carey A. Moore, "On the Origins of the LXX Additions to the Book of Esther," *Journal of Biblical Literature* 92 (1973): 382–393 offers a brief but helpful study on the LXX additions alone. For more thorough studies of the textual history of the book of Esther, see D.J.A. Clines, *The Esther Scroll: The Story of the Story,* Journal for the Study of the Old Testament Supplement Series 30 (Sheffield: JSOT, 1984); Michael V. Fox, *The Redaction of the Book of Esther: On Reading Composite Texts,* Society of Biblical Literature Monograph Series 40 (Atlanta: Scholars Press, 1991); Karen H. Jobes, *The Alpha-Text of Esther: Its Character and Relationship to the Masoretic Text,* Society of Biblical Literature Dissertation Series 153 (Atlanta: Scholars Press, 1996).

[2] E.g., Clines, *Esther Scroll,* 109.

[3] E.g., David A. deSilva, *Introducing the Apocrypha: Message, Content, and Significance* (Grand Rapids: Baker Academic, 202), 115.

[4] See, e.g., Ralph W. Klein, *Textual Criticism of the Old Testament: From the Septuagint to Qumran* (Philadelphia: Fortress Press, 1974), 74–75.

the origin of other readings; in this case, a book without God in its original explains why translators would add him far easier than the other way around.[5] Besides the analogy of the principles of textual criticism, deSilva offers another strong argument for the secondary nature of the additions. Although he acknowledges that four of the additions are consistent with Palestinian Jewish and apocalyptic literature, he concludes that without the additions, the story remains a coherent whole; with them, unnecessary contradictions are introduced into a formerly consistent narrative.[6] Moore says that the internal evidence of the letters (Additions B and E) is "much too florid and rhetorical in character to be anything but Greek in origin."[7] In addition, Moore offers external evidence for their secondary character: none of the Semitic translations based on the Hebrew text has them (viz., the Talmud, Targumim, and Syriac); Origen mentions that neither the prayers of Esther and Mordecai nor the letters of Haman and Mordecai appeared in the Hebrew texts of his day; Jerome noted they were not in the Hebrew texts of his day and relocated them to the end of the narrative; Josephus does not include Additions A and F in his paraphrase of the story; and the additions (and some canonical portions) are not present in Aquila, Symmachus, or Theodotion.[8]

---

[5] Clines does not explain why he believes the author would omit religious language. Robert Pfeiffer, *History of New Testament Times, with an Introduction to the Apocrypha* (New York: Harper & Brothers, 1949), 309–310 argues it was removed as a safeguard against blasphemy while the scroll was read during the heavy drinking at Purim. While this might explain why God's name was removed from the scroll, it does not explain the need to edit out references to prayer or other religious features (David deSilva, email message to author, June 27, 2015).

[6] deSilva, *Introducing the Apocrypha*, 115.

[7] Carey A. Moore, *Daniel, Esther and Jeremiah: The Additions: A New Translation with Introduction and Commentary,* The Anchor Bible (Garden City: Doubleday and Company, Inc., 1977), 154. See below for discussion of the additions.

[8] Ibid., 153–154.

If it is true that the religious language was added, this represents the first stage in the history of Esther's interpretation. It seems, then, that the same sort of questions that trouble modern readers about the absence of God and the morality of the heroes troubled earlier readers as well. Thus, translators turned the story into an exemplary tale where the actions of Esther and Mordecai are unquestionably noble and orthodox.[9] I will provide an overview of the additions below, which will show how the translators added religious elements to the narrative.

### 1. Additions

The following is a summary of the additions shared between the LXX and AT of Esther.[10]

*a. Addition A* comes before Esther 1. It introduces Mordecai and tells of a dream he had about two dragons that were "ready to fight." One of the dragons and all the nations prepared to fight against "the righteous nation." The righteous nation calls out to God and is delivered by a tiny spring that becomes a great river, bringing about the downfall of the unjust. Upon awakening from the dream, Mordecai hears of a plot against the king's life and warns him.[11] Mordecai is rewarded and promoted (thus

---

[9] Barry G. Webb, *Five Festal Garments: Christian Reflections on the Song of Songs, Ruth, Lamentations, Ecclesiastes, and Esther,* New Studies in Biblical Theology (Downers Grove: Inter-Varsity Press, 2000), 120.

[10] Jerome's relocation of the additions to the end of Esther in the Vulgate led to earlier English translations placing them there as well, though they make little sense at the end of the story. Modern Bibles with the apocrypha (e.g., the RSV and NRSV) have placed the additions in their proper place in the narrative.

[11] In the LXX Ahasuerus is identified with Artaxerxes instead of Xerxes. Ahasuerus, however, is the Hebrew form of the Persian name *Khshayarshan* which was transliterated into Greek and then Anglicized to "Xerxes." See, e.g., Michael V. Fox, *Character and Ideology in the Book of Esther* (Grand Rapids: Eerdmans, 1991), 14. Lewis Bales Paton, *A Critical and Exegetical Commentary on the Book of Esther,* The International Critical Com-

explaining at the outset his position at the gate of the city) and Haman, who favored the conspirators, is displeased and decides to do harm to both Mordecai and his people (thus explaining the hostility against the Jews and the conflict with Haman, and giving Esther a purpose in replacing Vashti).

*b. Addition B* is placed after Esther 3.13. It contains the contents of Haman's edict, saying the Jews are antagonistic to society and that, in his benevolence, the king wants to unify his kingdom by removing them.

*c. Addition C* is added after Esther 4.17, and so follows Esther's decision to see the king unbidden. It tells of two prayers, one by Mordecai and the other by Esther. Mordecai's prayer acknowledges God as sovereign creator and explains that he did not bow to Haman because he would only bow to God. It also emphasizes God's covenant with Israel by reference to the Abrahamic covenant and Exodus. Esther's prayer speaks of the election of Israel and requests strength and courage as she readies herself to appear before the king. She also explains that she abhors the bed of the uncircumcised king, has kept kosher, avoided participating in idolatry, and despises her position like a menstrual rag.

*d. Addition D* significantly expands upon and "is woven within" the MT of Esther 5.1–2.[12] It refers back to Esther's prayer and explicitly says God was in control of the king's attitude. In

---

mentary (Edinburgh: T&T Clark, 1908), 51–53 points out that every Persian king "from Cyaxares to Artaxerxes Ochus" had been suggested for the identity of Ahasuerus until the Persian monuments were deciphered, where Xerxes' name "appears in such a form as to leave no doubt that he is the king who is meant by Ahasuerus."

[12] Karen H Jobes and Moisés Silva, *Invitation to the Septuagint* (Grand Rapids: Baker Academic, 2000), 228. They go on to argue that the identical interweaving of the LXX and AT (in addition to the "cut-and-paste" nature of the other five additions) suggests they were copied from one Greek version to the other.

addition to bringing God to the text, in the reshaped literary structure of Esther (due to the additions), Addition D becomes the center of the book.[13]

e. *Addition E* is placed after Esther 8.12. It gives the contents of Mordecai's counter-edict. It is comparable to Haman's edict (Addition B) but contains political and theological language. Haman is called a Macedonian who is trying to weaken the Persian Empire by plotting against Artaxerxes from inside. The Jews are called "children of the living God, most high, most mighty"; their enemies are said to be trying to escape "the evil-hating justice of God"; and Haman's death sentence was said to be brought about by "God, who rules over all things." God is also credited with delivering "his chosen people." Mordecai's edict about Purim includes the directive that the festival is to be kept "to God."

f. *Addition F* closes the narrative, following Esther 10.4. It interprets the dream of Addition A: Mordecai and Haman were the two dragons; the peoples prepared to attack the Jews were the nations, and help from God came through Esther, who was the stream of water. Together with Addition A, Addition F clearly makes God the active participant behind the scenes[14] and clarifies that "God has determined in advance the outcome of this story and will be at work to bring about the end that God has chosen."[15]

---

[13] deSilva, *Introducing the Apocrypha*, 113.

[14] Jobes, *The Alpha-Text of Esther*, 184–185.

[15] deSilva, *Introducing the Apocrypha*, 112.

## 2. Other Changes

In addition to these major additions, there are smaller modifications of the Hebrew text in the LXX and AT that "introduce the overt acts and oversight of God into the story."[16]

*a. Esther 2.20 (LXX).* Esther 2.20 in the MT says Esther had not made her kindred or her people known, as Mordecai commanded her. The LXX adds that part of Mordecai's instruction was to fear God and keep his laws.[17]

*b. Esther 4.8 (LXX).* In Esther 4.8, Mordecai sends Haman's decree to Esther by Hathach the eunuch, commanding her to go to the king and plead for her people. The LXX specifically includes prayer in this instruction ("Call on the Lord").

*c. Esther 4.14, 16 (AT).*[18] Mordecai's argument to Esther in chapter 4 includes the vague reference to "another place" from which salvation will come (v 14).[19] To that end, Esther commands that Mordecai gather the people for a fast (v 16). The AT clarifies the enigmatic "another place" by saying God would be their help and salvation, and it replaces the reference to fasting with a service of worship and prayer.

*d. Esther 6.1 (LXX; AT).* The king's coincidental insomnia is clarified as the work of God. The LXX says that God took sleep from him; the AT says that "the mighty one" did.

---

[16] Ibid., 110. Those modifications listed follow Dunne's listing, noting only those with explicitly religious overtones. See deSilva, *Introducing the Apocrypha*, 113–114 for a more detailed discussion of all the minor changes.

[17] The AT does not mention Esther hiding her identity or Mordecai's instruction for her to do so.

[18] There is no standard versification of the AT. The Cambridge and Göttingen editions are different from each other, and both are different from the LXX and MT. For the sake of simplicity, where an AT addition is discussed, the verse listed is the corresponding MT verse.

[19] See page 72n55, below, for a further discussion of "another place" and various interpretations of the nature of Mordecai's statement.

*e. Esther 6.13 (LXX).* Zeresh's statement that Haman would fall before Mordecai because of his Jewishness is lengthened to include the reason: "because the living God is with him."

*f. Esther 7.2 (AT).* The AT says God gave Esther courage before her conformation with Haman at the second banquet.

*g. Esther 8.17 (LXX; AT).* Following Mordecai's counter-edict and his public appearance as grand vizier, fear of the Jews fell on the people and many declared themselves to be Jews. Both the LXX and AT specify this as a reference to circumcision, though in the LXX the Gentiles are circumcised and in the AT the Jews circumcise themselves.

### 3. Summary

While there are clear differences between the LXX and MT in a variety of Old Testament books, none are quite as dramatic as the book of Esther, which was altered by the translators in a manner and to an extent that no other canonical book was.[20] It seems clear that the secular nature of the book of Esther was as much a scandal to the early audiences as it is to some modern readers. It has been suggested that it was the marginal status of Esther within the Hebrew canon that made the translators comfortable with making such emendations, hoping, perhaps, to make it more worthy of its sacred status.[21] To that end, God was added—not only in places where his absence seemed most conspicuous (e.g., 4.14–16), but throughout the narrative.[22]

---

[20] deSilva, *Introducing the Apocrypha*, 115.

[21] Ibid.

[22] Louis A. Brighton, "The Book of Esther—Textual and Canonical Considerations," *Concordia Journal* 13 no. 3 (1987): 212 says that the LXX can serve as commentary on the MT to help the reader "see explicitly what is already implied in the canonical text."

# B. Jewish Interpretation[23]

### 1. Josephus

Josephus' reading of the story of Esther also reflects religious additions. Based on his attribution of the story to the time of Artaxerxes (*Antiquities* 11.6.1), it seems Josephus likely had access to the LXX version of Esther. Mostly, Josephus retells the basic storyline of Esther with intermittent references to God and religious practices included.[24]

For example, Mordecai's statement of salvation arising from "another place" is clarified to say help would certainly arise from God in some other way (11.6.7). Mordecai, along with the people, beseeches God not to overlook his nation at this time of imminent destruction, but that, as he provided for them and forgave them in the past, so would he now deliver them again (11.6.8). Furthermore, Mordecai clarifies that he did not bow to Haman, because it would have been to worship him, and it was this that had caused Haman's anger to arouse against them (11.6.8). Esther also prayed for God to have mercy on her, to make her words persuasive and her countenance more beautiful than before, for the sake of winning the king's favor (11.6.8).

Upon her arrival, the king looks at Esther severely and "with a countenance on fire with anger ... but the king changed

---

[23] This section primarily focuses on the religious additions to the narrative and will not examine every detail of Jewish interpretation, such as the supposed marriage of Mordecai and Esther (see, e.g., Barry Dov Walfish, "Kosher Adultery? The Mordecai-Esther-Ahasuerus Triangle in Midrash and Exegesis," *Prooftexts* 22 [2002]: 305–333 for one summary of that particular issue).

[24] It is hard to know whether Josephus' religious statements reflect the LXX's influence or the same sort of religious additions the Rabbis made in midrash and many Christian preachers make in sermons from Esther. As noted above, Additions A and F are not in Josephus' summary, though this may have more to do with his purposes in writing than their presence or lack thereof in the copy of Esther Josephus had.

his mind, which happened, as I suppose, by the will of God"
(11.6.9). After the first banquet, Zeresh advises Haman to build
the gallows, and God laughs, delighted at how he knew the
events would turn out. God then took away the king's sleep to
prepare the way for that reversal (11.6.10). Then, after the humiliation of chapter 6, Zeresh and the friends tell Haman he
will never overcome Mordecai, for God is with him.

Mordecai's counter-edict also contains references to God.
He says the punishment which befell Haman was sent upon
him by God and that God had made 13 Adar a day of salvation
(11.6.12). Finally, in the letter instituting Purim, the people are
called upon to observe the days and give thanks to God on them
(11.6.13). So we can see, for Josephus, it was clear that God was
acting throughout the course of the narrative.

## 2. Rabbinics

a. *Midrashim.* The Rabbis also added religious elements to the
Esther story, but they did so through midrashic exegesis of
the MT.[25] Midrashic readings of a text can seem "unabashedly
anachronistic and delightfully fanciful,"[26] perhaps nowhere
more so than in Esther. For example, in the midrashim, Ahasuerus and Vashti are vilified; Mordecai and Esther are made
pious; the golden vessels used for drinking at the party were
from the Jerusalem Temple; Vashti's party is in the king's bedroom; Haman's daughter dumps the contents of a chamber
pot onto Haman's head; Mordecai forces Haman to bathe him

---

[25] Adele Berlin, *Esther,* The JPS Bible Commentary (Philadelphia: The Jewish Publication Society, 2001), liii.

[26] Ibid. There is, however, much more to midrashim than mere fanciful interpretation. See, e.g., Martin Pickup, "New Testament Interpretation of the Old Testament: The
Theological Rationale of Midrashic Exegesis," *Journal of the Evangelical Theological Society*
51 no. 2 (2008): 353–381.

and then uses Haman's neck as a leg-up to the king's horse; and other fanciful ideas. As Berlin says, the midrashim clearly do not reflect a plain reading of the story but imaginatively enrich it.[27]

*b. Targumim.* In addition to the midrashim, there are two targumim of Esther, Aramaic translations and expansions on the text.[28] In *Targum Rishon*, Esther is a descendant of Sarah (1.1), which may be intended to contrast the unsavory characters Mordecai is introduced with (i.e., Shimei and Jeconiah). The banquet attendees use utensils from the Jerusalem temple (1.7), but Mordecai is not in attendance because he is fasting and praying (1.7, 10). Mordecai's name is associated with myrrh (2.5; rather than Marduk?), and Shimei is allowed to live for so long after David's curse because he foresaw the birth of Esther and Mordecai (2.5). Mordecai's refusal to bow is also clarified: Haman had an image of a god on his chest, so to bow to him would be idolatrous (3.2). Esther 4 is seen as a scene of repentance for the Jews participating in the king's feast (4.1), and God is twice called "the Lord of the Universe," both when Mordecai says deliverance will come from him and when Esther implores the people to pray to him during the fast (4.14, 16). The connection to Passover is twice made—in relation to the fast which transgresses the Passover (4.17) and on the third day of it when Esther appears before the king (5.1). Esther also prays before going to the king, though her prayer is significantly different from the one reported in the LXX: here, we learn Haman wanted the king to marry his daughter but, according

---

[27] Berlin, *Esther,* liv.

[28] Ibid., liii says they are the most expansive of all the targumim: "[I]t is stretching a point to call them translations; they are better labeled midrashim." Paton, *Esther,* 100–102 goes so far as to call the LXX and Josephus midrashim as well.

to the decree of Heaven, "each day she became defiled with excrement and with urine," and "her mouth smelled exceedingly offensive," which is why Esther wound up marrying him (5.1). The Jews study the law, circumcise their children, and wear phylacteries (8.16), and the enemies defeated were specifically named as Amalekites (9.13).

*Targum Sheni* is significantly different from *Targum Rishon*, which might reflect the moral ambiguity of Esther and the various ways it could be clarified.[29] In this targum, Mordecai went back to Jerusalem but was exiled again (2.6). He attempted to hide Esther, protecting her from the king's decree to bring in all the virgins (2.8). Mordecai explains his refusal to bow as loyalty to God, to whom alone he would bow, and he offers a doxology, praising God for his creation (3.3). Mordecai calls on the people to repent, urging the people to consider the repentance of the Ninevites in the Jonah story (4.1). Esther's thirty-day absence from the king's presence is explained as being due to her constant prayer over that time that she not be summoned to go before him and sin with him (4.11). Mordecai's "another place" is clarified as "their Holy One and Redeemer" (4.14), and Esther expresses confidence in an afterlife (4.16). She prays before going to the king, recalling the salvation of Shadrach, Meshach, and Abednego (5.1). The end of the story contains another doxology to God for his deliverance (8.15).

### 3. Medieval Interpretation

Following the influence of Anan ben David (715–795), who did not believe rabbinic writings to be authoritative, Sa'adia

---

[29] Dunne, *Esther and Her Elusive God*, 78.

ben Joseph (882–942) interpreted the Hebrew Bible with a clear, literal meaning and offered commentary that advocates for the natural grammatical reading.[30] Solomon ben Isaac (i.e., Rashi; 1040–1105) was the founder of the *peshaṭ* (literal) school of interpretation in Europe and is one of the most influential Rabbis to this day. Rashi first sought the literal interpretation of a text, though he did not entirely break with midrashic exegesis; rather, he used it only when it did not conflict with the literal meaning.[31] Abraham ibn Ezra (1089–1167), another of the most influential Rabbis and an advocate of *peshaṭ*, composed a commentary on Esther that could be found in Rabbinic Bibles for many years.[32]

In the 13th century, Jewish interpretation took a new form as it borrowed from Christians the fourfold sense of Scripture. The Jewish exegetes adopted the following doctrine: the *peshaṭ* (simple meaning); the *midrash* (traditional meaning); the *Ḥokhma* (philosophic meaning); and the *Cabala* (mystical, allegorical meaning). After this method became mainstream, nearly all commentaries followed it, and the last method—Cabala—was preferred. While Paton calls this "the death of genuine exegesis,"[33] it is striking that the allegorical method dominated multiple religions for hundreds of years. While allegory may tend toward fanciful interpretations and the allegorist perhaps needs to take extra care in applying the method to Scripture, it is over-

---

[30] Paton, *Esther*, 104–105. Paton is the only source I have found that discusses these interpreters, and he still gives little-to-no information on their actual interpretation of the text of Esther. Thus, this section only details a few of the medieval Jewish interpreters and the general approach to the text they take.

[31] Ibid., 105.

[32] Ibid., 106.

[33] Ibid.

statement to say it has no purpose, especially when New Testament authors, at least on occasion, use allegory to interpret the Old Testament (e.g., Gal 4.21–31).

### 4. Summary

Early Jewish interpretation of Esther universally seeks to add religion to the story: faith and piety are emphasized; Esther's presence in the pagan court is either downplayed or justified; and, very often, conflict or hostility is introduced to the story before the competition.[34] As Dunne says, "[T]he protagonists are made into religious and moral exemplars, the rough parts are smoothed over, and the parts that are meant to make readers blush are childproofed."[35] It seems clear that the apparently secular nature of the story bothered the ancient Jewish interpreters, so they sought to edit it.

## C. Christian Interpretation

### 1. Church Fathers

The early church essentially ignored the book of Esther.[36] In the West, only Clement of Rome (first century) and Hippolytus (third) refer to it, and neither indicate whether or not it is regarded as Scripture. In the East, Melito (second) excluded it from his list of canonical books, but Origen (second/third) included it. Clement of Alexandria (third) also included it, and gave us a clue to how he read it, saying Esther clothed herself "mystically"

---

[34] Dunne, *Esther and Her Elusive God,* 84–89.

[35] Ibid., 91.

[36] The following paragraph summarizes Roger Beckwith, *The Old Testament Canon of the New Testament Church and its Background in Early Judaism* (London: SPCK, 1985), 296–308.

as a type of redemption.[37] Beyond this, there are passing references to Esther in sermons, but no Christian commentaries on Esther were written during the first seven centuries.[38]

## 2. Medieval Interpretation and the Reformers

A few medieval commentaries were written on Esther, though none are exegetical; they are all homiletical or devotional and use an allegorical method.[39]

The Reformers took a variety of approaches to Esther. Calvin apparently ignored the book of Esther, never preaching from it nor writing a commentary on it.[40] Luther, however, was not so kind as to ignore it. He famously expressed hostility toward it, saying he wished it did not exist, because it contained too much Judaizing and heathen perversity.[41]

In addition to these more familiar names, Sebastian Münster, Johannes Drusius, and Hugo Grotius are among the more important Reformation commentators on Esther.[42] They assume Esther to be strictly historical and discuss matters such

---

[37] *Paedagogue* 3.12.5.

[38] Paton, *Esther*, 101.

[39] Ibid., 107.

[40] Although Calvin wrote commentaries prolifically, he only covered 24 of the 39 Old Testament books. Notably, he did not write on most of the historical books, including all three post-exilic histories. It is, thus, hard to know whether he intentionally excluded Esther from his writings or just never got to it.

[41] Martin Luther, *Table Talk* 22.2080. By contrast, Webb, *Five Festal Garments*, 130 suggests the Judaizing that Luther objects to is precisely what makes the book of Esther invaluable: God's commitment to the survival of Israel. This does not, however, imply what Brevard Childs, *Introduction to the Old Testament as Scripture* (Minneapolis: Augsburg Fortress, 1979), 298 says, i.e, that Esther's inclusion in the canon "serves as a check against all attempts to spiritualize the concept of Israel—usually by misinterpreting Paul—and thus removing the ultimate scandal of biblical particularity."

[42] See Paton, *Esther*, 108 for a fuller list of Esther commentaries of the Reformation period.

as Ahasuerus' right to divorce Vashti; Esther's right to marry Ahasuerus; Mordecai's justification in telling Esther to conceal her identity; Esther's eating of the king's food; the morality of the Jews killing their enemies; and other such moral questions, showing the religious nature of Esther continued to be a key interpretive issue.[43]

---

[43] Paton, *Esther,* 108.

# TWO

## Key Interpretive Issues

With the history of interpretation briefly sketched out, we turn to what are some of the key interpretive issues. In this chapter, two will be discussed. First, the question of Esther's canonicity will be investigated. This seems to be very closely related to the lack of any explicit religious element in Esther. Second, we will consider the dual questions of historicity and genre, two related matters that dominate much discussion in modern commentaries.

It should be noted that a third key interpretive issue is not discussed in this chapter, namely the question of God and religion in Esther. If you have looked at the table of contents, you already know why that is: it is given an entire section of the book and comprises the largest portion of this work.

### A. Canonicity

A matter closely related to the religious interpretation of Esther is the question of canonicity. Esther has long been one of the most debated books of the Bible, as it relates to the question of its inclusion in the canon. Although there is little specific information given about why it was so hotly debated, some reasonable guesses can be made. Moore suggests the following: the lack of religious elements; the questionable historicity of the narrative; and the possibility of Purim first being a non-Jewish festival.[1] These last two matters, however, may be reading a modern scholarly debate back into an ancient world. There is little evidence that early readers of Esther saw it as non-historical. Without that evidence, one would be hard pressed to prove early Jews (or Christians) saw Purim as originally a non-Jewish festival. While some Jews may have chafed at it being non-Mosaic, it is most likely that the absence of God or the covenant was the primary driving force behind the questions.

## 1. Jewish Perspectives

The Qumran community apparently did not consider Esther to be canonical; it is the only Old Testament text not found among their library.[2] Josephus apparently accepts Esther's canonicity, because he argues for 22 canonical books.[3] By AD 90, the question seemed to have been resolved since the Council of Jamnia included it in its canonical list. The issue, however, apparently persisted as Melito (AD 170) did not include Esther in a list of books the Jews of the East believed to be canonical. Additionally, two passages from the Talmud show some Jews did not regard Esther to be canonical (literally, "as defiling the

---

[1] Moore, *Daniel, Esther, and Jeremiah: The Additions*, 156.

[2] As Moore, *Esther*, xxi notes, this may be merely an archaeological accident. Like all arguments from silence, it is tenuous, at best. However, the fact that they did not include Purim in their festival calendar gives some credence to the perspective that it was intentionally omitted from their collection.

[3] *Against Apion* 1.8.861–862. Josephus' 22 canonical books correspond to our 39 Old Testament books: the twelve Minor Prophets were counted as a single book, as were Samuel, Kings, Chronicles, Judges-Ruth, Ezra-Nehemiah, and Jeremiah-Lamentations.

hands").[4] Yet once its canonicity was established, it became an extremely important book to the Jews, as Purim became one of the most important festivals of the Jewish calendar.[5]

## 2. *Christian Perspectives*

It was no easier for Christians to come to a consensus on the matter of Esther's canonicity than for the Jews. Generally speaking, the Christians in the West accepted it, while those in the East often did not, though I have not discovered a reason for the geographical discrepancy. Even those who did accept it in the East often did so tentatively, making it the last book in their canonical listing.[6] That it was frequently associated with Judith by the Fathers,[7] a book denied canonical status by Jews and Christians, did not help its case. Ultimately, Esther was included in the canonical lists produced at the Council of Hippo (AD 393) and the Council of Carthage (AD 397).

With regard to the additions to Esther, their canonicity divides along the Catholic/Protestant line: Protestants have rejected them as apocryphal; Catholics, following the Council of Trent, have accepted them as deuterocanonical.[8]

---

[4] See Moore, *Esther,* xxiv for the full Talmud quotes. Counterintuitively, the Talmud says that Scripture defiles the hands and uninspired books do not.

[5] Frederic W. Bush, *Ruth, Esther,* Word Biblical Commentary (Nashville: Thomas Nelson, 1996), 276. Carey A. Moore, "Eight Questions Most Frequently Asked About the Book of Esther," *Bible Review* 3 (1987): 29 points to Maimonides (AD 1135–1204), who ranked Esther second only to the Torah and the high number of medieval manuscripts of the *megillah* as evidence of its later popularity.

[6] See Moore, *Esther,* xxv for a full listing of Church Fathers who denied its canonicity from the late 200s through the early 800s as well as those who accepted it from the fourth century onward. One notable example is Athanasius, who listed Esther as among seven non-canonical books that qualifies as edifying reading "for instruction in the word of godliness" (*Festal Letters,* 39).

[7] E.g., 1 Clement 55.

[8] See Moore, *Daniel, Esther, and Jeremiah: The Additions,* 155–156.

## 3. Jesus' View

To the Christian, Jesus' view of the book of Esther is more significant than human councils, whether held by Christians in the fourth century or Rabbis in the first. Although he never specifically addresses the issue of the Old Testament canon, his silence on questionable books may be telling. If it may be reasonably presumed Jesus had access to the same canon as Josephus,[9] then his various references to the authority of Scripture (e.g., Matt 5.17–18)—and his (and his apostles') apparent lack of any concern that the Hebrew canon was in error—may indicate that, in his judgment, the Old Testament canon was fixed.[10]

## B. Historicity and Genre

Two topics that have dominated the interpretation of Esther since the early 20th century are historicity and the closely related question of genre, topics too significant for a discussion of interpretation to ignore. Although these issues are not as closely tied to the religious interpretation of the book of Esther, which is the primary focus of this book, they are at least peripherally related. For example, while there is not a complete correlation and the inverse is not necessarily true, those who take a historical view of the text tend also to take its canonicity for granted and argue God is present throughout the narrative.

---

[9] The presumption that Jesus had access to the same Hebrew canon can be deduced by his reference to the first and last martyrs in the Hebrew canonical order, which did not match the LXX (Luke 11.51) and his familiarity with the three-part division of the Hebrew Bible (Luke 24.44). See, e.g., Neil R. Lightfoot, *How We Got the Bible* (Grand Rapids: Baker Books, 2003), 153–154.

[10] See Martin Pickup, "Canonicity of the Bible," *Reemphasizing Bible Basics,* Florida College Annual Lectures (Temple Terrace: Florida College Bookstore, 1990), 166–169.

## 1. Historicity

For centuries, Esther was assumed to be a historical narrative, though that view has come under fire since the publication of Paton's commentary in 1908. Overall, opinions vary—from Paton, who doubts whether there is even a historical kernel underlying the narrative,[11] to Keil, who argues for its complete historicity,[12] to Moore, who points out historical concurrences and historical difficulties and says that it could be essentially true.[13] The greatest difficulty in navigating this matter is that scholars on either side tend to speak past each other: many who adhere to its historicity merely seek to answer each objection, presuming that to do so proves its historicity and, in turn, they overstate their conclusions;[14] meanwhile, some who argue against its historicity merely list objections and conclude its fictitious nature without ever critically interacting with potentially plausible solutions.[15]

Those who argue for its historicity point to the hallmarks of historical narrative it contains.[16] For the most part, it reads as

---

[11] E.g., Paton, *Esther*, 131–139. David G. Firth, "The Third Quest for the Historical Mordecai and the Genre of the Book of Esther," *Old Testament Essays* 16 no. 2 (2003): 236 points out that Paton takes an either/or stance on whether the book is history or fiction because it does not conform to sober research, but makes no positive argument for it being a work of fiction, nor does he raise the possibility that it is simply poorly written history.

[12] E.g., Carl Friedrich Keil, "Esther," *Commentary on the Old Testament* (Peabody, Mass.: Hendrickson, 1996), 191–195.

[13] C.A. Moore, "Archaeology and the Book of Esther," *Biblical Archaeologist* 38 (1975): 68. See also C.A. Moore, "Eight Questions Most Asked about the Book of Esther," *Biblical Review* 3 (1987): 16–31.

[14] To Breneman's credit, he acknowledges that there is a stark difference between answering difficulties and proving historicity. Mervin Breneman, *Ezra, Nehemiah, Esther*, The New American Commentary (Nashville: Broadman & Holman, 1993), 280.

[15] E.g., Jon D. Levenson, *Esther: A Commentary*, The Old Testament Library (Louisville: Westminster John Knox, 1997), 23–27.

[16] See J. Stafford Wright, "The Historicity of the Book of Esther," *New Perspectives*

a historical narrative; for example, it has chronological references (1.1; 2.16; 3.7, 13; 8.9; 9.1) and includes reference to the chronicles of the king (2.23; 6.1; 10.2).[17] Further, nearly all scholars have noted its description of the Persian palace at Susa reflects remarkable knowledge of the court[18] and the general descriptions of Ahasuerus fit well with what is known from Herodotus.[19] Finally, many point to the etiological aspect of Esther as noteworthy. It probably overstates the matter to say there is "no other reasonable explanation for the historic fact of the Feast of Purim" than such a deliverance as described in the book of Esther actually happening.[20] There is, however, merit in thinking about the historical question in terms of the exis-

---

*on the Old Testament* ed. J.B. Payne (Waco: Word Books, 1970), 37–47; William H. Shea, "Esther and History," *Concordia Journal* 13 no. 3 (1987): 234–248; and Forrest S. Weiland, "Historicity, Genre, and Narrative Design in the Book of Esther" *Bibliotheca Sacra* 159 (2002): 151–165 for thoroughgoing arguments for its historicity.

[17] Weiland, "Historicity, Genre, and Narrative Design," 156–158. More debated is the book's opening וַיְהִי ("Now it took place," NASB), which has been pointed to as evidence of historical writing (e.g., Joyce G. Baldwin, *Esther: An Introduction and Commentary,* Tyndale Old Testament Commentaries [Downers Grove: Inter-Varsity Press, 1984], 16; Weiland, "Hitoricity, Genre, and Narrative Design," 156) and as evidence of its legendary quality (e.g., Timothy K. Beal, "Esther," *Ruth and Esther,* Berit Olam Studies in Hebrew Narrative and Poetry [Collegeville: The Liturgical Press, 1999], 3).

[18] See, e.g., Edwin Yamauchi "The Archaeological Background of Esther," *Bibliotheca Sacra* 137 (1980): 110 and Yamauchi, "Mordecai, The Persepolis Tablets, and The Susa Excavations," *Vetus Testamentum* 42 no. 2 (1992): 272–274.

[19] C.A. Moore, "Archaeology and the Book of Esther," 69; In particular, Yamauchi, "Archaeological Background," 104 says that Herodotus "presents an unflattering portrait of the king as an impatient, hot-tempered monarch with a wandering eye for women." cf. Edwin M. Yamauchi, *Persia and the Bible* (Grand Rapids: Baker Book House, 1990), 228–229.

[20] Gleason Archer, *A Survey of Old Testament Introduction* (Chicago: Moody Press, 1974), 421. Cf. Siegfried H. Horn, "Mordecai, A Historical Problem," *Biblical Research* 9 (1964): 16 who says that Purim "must have a historical background" and points to its connection to Mordecai as early as 2 Maccabees and Josephus' connection of Purim with the events of Esther.

tence of Purim, especially since there are no extant competing etiologies of Purim.

In addition to these general principles, there are some matters that are generally beyond dispute as pointing to Esther's historicity.[21] These include the book's knowledge of the extent of Xerxes' Empire, from Ethiopia to India;[22] how the banquet of Esther 1 corresponds to the Xerxes' pre-invasion council of 483 BC; the author's knowledge of Persia;[23] and the use of Persian terms for objects and names, nearly all of which have been found in Persian texts.[24]

*a. Alleged Historical Inaccuracies.* There are, however, difficulties with Esther's historicity. Below are some of the common objections raised as well as some of the standard answers provided.[25]

i. Number of Provinces. The book of Esther enumerates 127 provinces in the Persian Empire, but Herodotus only reports 20 satrapies (3.89). Skeptics of Esther's historicity often make no distinction between provinces and satrapies, suggesting it

---

[21] David M. Howard, *An Introduction to the Historical Books* (Chicago: Moody Press, 1993), 319–320.

[22] But see below on the numbering of the provinces/satrapies.

[23] This includes more than the palace details mentioned above. For example, although Paton, *Esther,* 72 says that decrees were not ordinarily published in the languages of the provinces, but Aramaic, Kenneth Kitchen, *On the Reliability of the Old Testament* (Grand Rapids: Eerdmans, 2003), 76 points to multiple texts that have been found illustrating decrees and documents written in the script and language of each province. The Persian postal system is another oft cited element of Persian culture that is accurately portrayed in Esther.

[24] On names, see esp. Yamauchi, "Mordecai, The Persepolis Tablets, and the Susa Excavations," 273–274 and A.R. Millard, "The Persian Names in Esther and the Reliability of the Hebrew Text," *Journal of Biblical Literature* 96 (1977): 481–48.

[25] See, e.g., Paton, *Esther,* 64–77; Fox, *Character and Ideology,* 131–139 for arguments against its historicity.

represents a gross inaccuracy.[26] It is, however, clear that there were subdivisions of the satrapies into smaller units, such as the province "Beyond the River" (Ezra 5.3, 8; Neh 1.3), which was part of a larger satrapy. The word used for "province" in Esther 1.1 (מְדִינָה) is the same word used of the smaller units in Ezra and Nehemiah. Herodotus does not report this unit or the number associated with it.

ii. Esther as Queen. A more significant question is the matter of Esther being queen, which presents a twofold problem. First, Herodotus (3.84) says the king must choose his wife from one of seven specific families, of which Esther was not one. The first problem goes away when it is realized that Darius, Xerxes, and Artaxerxes all married outside the seven, including Queen Amestris—the wife of Xerxes recorded by Herodotus.[27]

Second, there is no record of a Queen Esther while there is record of a Queen Amestris. This is more difficult than the lack of any record of a Queen Esther in Herodotus, who gives a fairly thorough reporting of Xerxes' reign. Given the timing of Artaxerxes' birth it is impossible to identify Amestris with Esther.[28] Due to Amestris' accompaniment of Xerxes on his Greek cam-

---

[26] E.g., Paton, *Esther,* 72. But see Fox, *Character and Ideology,* 15 for an argument from Esther for why the terms should be understood synonymously.

[27] Wright, "Historicity of the Book of Esther," 38; Herodotus 3.67, 87; 5.25; 7.61; Ctesias 13.51; Ron Zadok, "On the Historical Background of the Book of Esther," *Biblische Notizen* 24 (1984): 19.

[28] Wright, "Historicity of the Book of Esther," 40–41. Robert Gordis, "Religion, Wisdom and History in the Book of Esther: A New Solution to an Ancient Crux," *Journal of Biblical Literature* 100 no. 3 (1981): 384, however, argues that "Esther" could be a shortening of "Amestris," though he does not deal with the chronological problem Wright poses.

paign, which appears to be after Vashti's demotion[29] in Esther 1, it is also difficult to identify Amestris with Vashti.[30] Regardless of whether Amestris is to be identified with Vashti, Baldwin offers a plausible solution of how Esther could fit in: a secondary wife who would not jeopardize the official queen nor necessarily appear in historical record, though who could be accommodatingly called a queen.[31]

iii. Existence of Mordecai. While Esther's absence in Herodotus may be written off as her simply being a secondary wife, it is more difficult to explain the absence of Xerxes' non-Persian grand vizier. Although there is reference to a Marduka who was a high official in Susa[32] and evidence that Jews held significant governmental roles in Persian culture,[33] it is extremely difficult to identify Marduka with Mordecai. First, the connection to the chief Babylonian deity likely made the name extremely common. As Levenson says, "One might as well argue that the appearance of the name 'George' as a colonist in North America in the eighteenth century proves accurate the old story of Washington and the cherry tree."[34] While there is

---

[29] Yamauchi, *Persia and the Bible*, 231 argues that the text implies that Vashti was demoted in the harem, not that she was killed or divorced.

[30] See Wright, "Historicity of the Book of Esther," 41–42 for an attempt to leap the linguistic and historical hurdles of identifying them.

[31] Baldwin, *Esther*, 21. Cf. Gordis, "Religion, Wisdom and History in the Book of Esther," 385.

[32] Arthur Ungand, "Keilinschriftliche Beiträge zum Buch Ezra und Esther," *Zeitschrift für die alttestamentliche Wissenschaft* 58 (1940–1941): 240–244.

[33] Horn, "Mordecai: A Historical Problem," 23–25.

[34] Levenson, *Esther*, 24. On the other hand, Yamauchi, "Mordecai, The Persepolis Tablets, and the Susa Excavations," 273 points to only four other people who were known by that name (which is itself an argument from silence). Firth, "The Third Quest for the Historical Mordecai," 238n10 concludes on the basis of Yamauchi's data that Levenson's analogy is inappropriate, given the paucity of the name.

some hyperbole in Levenson's point, the underlying argument is sound: a name's appearance in an ancient record does not prove the Mordecai of the book of Esther.

Second, the Marduka in question was an administrative functionary of some kind.[35] While this might match well with Mordecai's early position at the king's gate,[36] it leaves open the question of why his promotion is not mentioned if it is indeed the same Mordecai. This brings to light the bigger issue: to presume the historicity of Esther's Mordecai merely from the presence of a similar name on a tablet begs the question of his historicity and official role at the gate.[37]

iv. Unalterable laws. The nature of the fixed laws of the Medes and Persians[38] is a matter of contention in both Esther and Daniel. It is often alleged that there is no extra-biblical evidence for such a thing, and it is an impossible way to run an empire. The latter point certainly seems to have merit—it would be an infuriating way to manage affairs. This, however, does not prove that it could not have happened since it is perhaps no more infuriating or self-satirizing than several-hundred page bills that no congressman reads before voting on! More significantly, there may be an example of an unalterable law in Diodorous Siculus

---

[35] The precise nature of the word is debated. See David J.A. Clines, "In Quest of the Historical Mordecai," *Vetus Testamentum* 41 no. 2 (1991): 134 for a brief discussion of the options.

[36] Gordis, "Religion, Wisdom and History in the Book of Esther," 384.

[37] Clines, "In Quest of the Historical Mordecai," 134n20. Clines goes on to argue from the tablet that the Marduka in question is probably not a resident of Susa. Clines overall argumentation is strong enough to sway Yamauchi from arguing that the identification is the scholarly consensus ("The Archaeological Background of Esther," *Bibliotheca Sacra* 127 [1980]: 107) to acknowledging that Clines's reappraisal "may well be correct" ("Mordecai, The Persepolis Tablets, and the Susa Excavations," 272).

[38] E.g., "[A]n edict written in the name of the king and sealed with the king's ring cannot be revoked" (8.12).

17.30, translated by Wright as, "It was not possible for what was done by the royal authority to be undone," [39] which may be connected to "the Law of the Persians" a few sentences earlier. If Wright's assessment of Siculus is correct, then there is at least one extra-Biblical example of unalterable laws. [40]

v. Summary. With the possible exception of Amestris' queenship, every historical question is based on silence or expectations of what is probable. [41] Wright goes so far as to call them "trivial," [42] and Dillard and Longman say other difficulties which are sometimes raised are "comparatively minor and even border on pettifogging." [43] In sum, the historical difficulties are worth considering but do not prove the case against Esther's historicity. Likewise, however, the answers provided by the conservative adherents to its historical character do not prove the other side. At best, they allow the narrative to remain historically plausible.

*b. Internal Improbabilities.* In addition to these matters of extra-biblical attestation, there are other matters in the narrative that cause some skeptics to doubt its historicity.

i. 180-day party. Like the unalterable laws, a half-year party seems like a foolish way to run an empire. [44] If, however, this banquet corresponds to Xerxes' planning session for his Greek

---

[39] Wright, "Historicity of the Book of Esther," 39–40.

[40] But is a single example sufficient to prove a long-standing imperial policy?

[41] Breneman, *Ezra, Nehemiah, Esther,* 285; Wright, "Historicity of the Book of Esther," 40.

[42] Wright, "Historicity of the Book of Esther," 40.

[43] Raymond B. Dillard and Tremper Longman III, *An Introduction to the Old Testament* (Grand Rapids: Zondervan, 1994), 192.

[44] Beal, xvi simultaneously calls into question both the killing and the drinking: "[T]he amount of blood spilled in the story is matched only by the amount of wine poured."

invasion,[45] it would explain both the duration and the emphasis on Xerxes showing off his wealth and power to inspire confidence in his people that such a war would be successful.[46] Also, there are other ways to read the text than as a consecutive 180-day banquet.[47] Even if it is a 180-day-long banquet, the text does not necessarily mean the entire empire stopped to have a party for that time.[48]

ii. Mordecai's Age. Mordecai is said to be too old to play such an influential role in the narrative. This alleged problem comes from the relative pronoun in Mordecai's genealogy (2.5–6). If it refers to Mordecai, then he was taken captive with Jeconiah, making him well over 100 years old—but the narrative gives no clue at all that he is so old. The simplest explanation, and one taken by several expositors, is that the pronoun refers not back to Mordecai, but to Kish, the closest antecedent in the list.

iii. Gathering of the maidens in droves. Paton lists the gathering of maidens as one of the matters so "intrinsically improbable" that it is difficult to believe it could be true.[49] However, Artaxerxes was said to have had 360 concubines in his harem who were replenished by gathering virgins from the land.[50] Further, Herodotus says 500 young boys were gathered each year and castrated to serve as eunuchs in the court (3.92).

---

[45] So argues Shea, "Esther and History," 236.

[46] Moore, *Esther,* 12.

[47] Breneman, *Ezra, Nehemiah, Esther,* 280–281 suggests that it may refer to two banquets 180 days apart or two descriptions of one banquet at the end of 180 days.

[48] See F.B. Huey, "Esther," *1 & 2 Kings, 1 & 2 Chronicles, Ezra, Nehemiah, Esther, Job,* The Expositor's Bible Commentary (Grand Rapids: Zondervan, 1988), 789.

[49] Paton, *Esther,* 73.

[50] Karen Jobes, *Esther,* The NIV Application Commentary (Grand Rapids: Zondervan, 1999), 94.

Against this background, Xerxes' gathering of virgins seems much less improbable.

iv. Extermination of an entire race. Some have argued that Haman's plan is an impossibility. While the mass genocide of an ethnic group might sound extreme, the historical reality of Auschwitz—and other historical acts of genocide—should be sufficient to take the wind from the sails of this argument.[51]

v. Gigantic gallows built overnight. Haman's construction of 50-cubit gallows[52] in such a short time is a problem for some. However, since it is only mentioned in direct dialogue—by Zeresh and Harbona the eunuch, and never verified by the narrator—it may well qualify as exaggeration rather than historical detail.[53]

vi. Exaggerations. Between the 127 provinces, the 180-day party, the dozen eunuchs sent to fetch one woman, the unalterable laws, the worldwide edicts in every language, the every-available-woman gathering, the year-long cosmetics, the 75-foot gallows, and the 75,000-person body count, it seems as if the narrative may engage in a touch of hyperbole. Beal argues that to call these things "'literary embellishments' is to understate them almost as radically as the text overstates them," and that the narrative is blending history-likeness and outlandishness "in truly remarkable ways."[54] Lumping all of these matters together certainly gives the

---

[51] Cf. Gordis, "Religion, Wisdom and History in the Book of Esther," 383 for other historical accounts of such massacres.

[52] The English translation of עֵץ as "gallows" is an unfortunate one, as it immediately conjures images of noose-tied rope-hangings. The word itself simply means tree, though could be used of poles on which slain bodies were exposed (BDB). In addition, both Herodotus (3.125, 129; 4.43) and excavated stone reliefs indicate that Persians impaled their victims on a stake.

[53] Wright, "Historicity of the Book of Esther," 39.

[54] Beal, "Esther," xvii. W. Scott Watson, "The Authenticity and Genuineness of the Book of Esther," *The Princeton Theological Review* 1 no. 1 (1903): 64 surprisingly says that

appearance of a "sometimes horribly unbelievable" story,[55] but looking at them on a more point-by-point basis can help. For example, if the province/satrapy distinction suggested above is legitimate, then it can remain historically accurate while having the narrative function of supplying a larger number in a chapter that clearly is employing the motif of excess. If the 180-day party is a war-planning banquet that is not merely a half-year of drinking, it seems far less excessive. The gathering of virgins has historical precedent, both in harems and eunuchs. The 75-foot gallows may be merely an exaggeration. When these easy matters are resolved, all that remains are a small group of oddities that may or may not be excessive on their own. This may be why Moore admits, "on the face of it, the story seems to be true. ... Nothing in the book seems improbable, let alone unbelievable."[56]

c. *Herodotus and Arguments from Silence.* A major problem with the argument against historicity is that it is invariably rooted in Herotodus' history and arguments from silence—both of which should be at least somewhat dubious. Herodotus is not a modern historian, which makes it suspect to use his records as such—yet this is what skeptics of Esther's historicity invariably do. In addition to useful data, he includes legend, tradition, and hearsay.[57] Giving his history *de facto* credibility above the biblical record is a questionable move.

Furthermore, Herodotus' history is not complete. Herodotus stops recording his history after Xerxes' return to Persia following the Greek campaign, which makes it an overstatement to say,

---

there is "nothing fabulous or absurd" in the narrative!

[55] Beal, "Esther," xvii.

[56] Moore, *Esther,* xxxv.

[57] Gordis, "Religion, Wisdom and History in the Book of Esther," 385.

for example, that Amestris remained queen. Nothing else is said of her in Herodotus until her son Artaxerxes takes the throne.[58] While it does not prove the historicity of the Esther narrative, this gap would conceivably allow for a time where Amestris (if she were Vashti) was not permitted into the king's presence. Ultimately, nearly all arguments against Esther's historicity come from the silences in Herodotus' record.[59] One would think that after the Belshazzar debacle,[60] critics would be more cautious about arguing based on what ancient history does not record.

Consequently, it is questionable whether the reader should immediately jump to the conclusion that the book of Esther is incorrect when it differs with Herodotus. As Hamilton says, "Historians have noted that Herodotus was not always the thorough, check-out-the-details-first researcher. Instead, he often relied on the rumor mill for his information, tidbits he picked up here and there."[61] As a result, Herodotus and his silences should not be the sole guide to the question of historicity.

---

[58] Shea, "Esther and History," 59.

[59] See Fox, *Character and Ideology*, 133n7 for a defense of the validity of arguments from silence when the event is of a certain magnitude and there are an adequate number of other sources that would have noted the event. Fox, however, begs the question. By contrast, many supposed biblical inaccuracies based on silence and an "adequate number of other sources" have been shown to be correct after all.

[60] Daniel's Belshazzar (Dan 5) was long thought to be a figment of the author's imagination, since no extrabiblical history mentioned him and "an adequate number of other sources" proved that Nabonidus was the last king of Babylon. Ultimately, archaeologists unearthed inscriptions that indicated Belshazzar was Nabonidus' eldest son and crown prince, and that he was entrusted with both the kingship and the army. In addition to showing his existence, it explains why Belshazzar offers the position of "third ruler in the kingdom" to the person able to interpret the handwriting on the wall (Dan 5.7). See, e.g., Alfred J. Hoerth, *Archaeology and the Old Testament* (Grand Rapids: Baker Books, 1998), 379–384.

[61] Victor Hamilton, *Handbook on the Historical Books* (Grand Rapids: Baker Academic, 2001), 532.

*d. Summary.* The question of historicity is difficult to answer. Several objections can be and have been raised and plausible answers are offered to most, if not all. The problem is that the objections alone do not disprove its historicity nor do the answers prove it.[62] To a large degree, the matter depends on one's starting point: does the reader embrace the apparent historical testimony unless there are compelling reasons not to or does the reader adopt a more skeptical stance, insisting the story must be proven historically true before accepting it?[63] The larger question is one of authorial intent, which leads to the related issue of genre.

## 2. Genre

However probable or plausible (or improbable or implausible) the above discussion may make the events of Esther, it does not provide a definitive conclusion about its historicity. As Fox notes, there are no definitive arguments *for* the historicity of Esther.[64] While extra-biblical attestation for every detail of every narrative should not be required for reasonable confidence in the trustworthiness of the narrative, there are multiple genres represented in the Bible, including some which are clearly fictitious that do not therefore demand a historical setting to make

---

[62] As a result, many have concluded that it has a "historical core," a point which Fox, *Character and Ideoogy,* 138 correctly points out "grant[s] that it is not historical as it stands."

[63] Iain Provan, et al, *A Biblical History of Israel* (Louisville: Westminster John Knox Press, 2003): 296–297.

[64] Fox, *Character and Ideology,* 134. The best one can offer is that the *conditions* are reasonably accurate. Even the historical accuracies do not prove the story of Esther, since, as Adele Berlin, "The Book of Esther and Ancient Storytelling," *Journal of Biblical Literature* 120 no. 1 (2001): 4 argues, "[T]o judge a story's historicity by its degree of realism is to mistake verisimilitude for historicity."

a theological point. Examples include Old and New Testament parables and, according to most scholars, the Song of Songs.[65] The question facing the exegete here, then, should not be how to defend Esther's historicity, but whether the book itself points in the direction of historical narrative or not: should effort be spent defending its historicity or should the interpreter simply seek the theological message contained therein? Since the exegete's primary purpose is not to interpret the text literally, but to interpret it appropriately, if the narrative itself points away from a historical reading, chasing a historical background misses the purpose of the narrative.

The genre question is an especially difficult one in Esther because there are clues pointing in a variety of directions. The presence of chronological references, invitations to search records, a specific historical setting, and an actual feast that claims to be derived from the events described in the book suggest it intends to be read as history. On the other hand, the presence of narrative design (conflict, escalation, turning point, climax, resolution) as well as other literary elements (such as irony, hyperbole, and satire) may point toward a non-historical account. At the same time, the literary elements just mentioned all have a certain comedic aspect to them, which might point toward burlesque[66] or farce.[67]

---

[65] Most approaches to the Song—whether allegory, drama, dream, or idealized love poetry—do not require or even suggest a historical setting; few argue that is speaks of a historical wedding of Solomon.

[66] Burlesque vulgarizes lofty material or treats ordinary material with mock dignity for the sake of laughter. See Berlin, *Esther,* xix.

[67] Farce employs extremely exaggerated or caricatured character types put in ludicrous situations. See Berlin, *Esther,* xix.

Due to this mixture of clues, a variety of perspectives has been suggested,[68] from straight history,[69] to novelistic history,[70] to a historical novel,[71] to pure fiction. This last view takes many forms, including the farce or burlesque view mentioned above[72] or a legendary etiology of Purim.[73] In the end, it is difficult to know Esther's genre for certain, though some principles can be suggested. First, literary character and narrative skill does not necessitate a fictional genre, nor do highly dramatic events need to be attributed to fiction.[74] Second, one's answer to the historicity question will likely be swayed by his or her conclusion on the genre question. For example, as Firth points out, the genre determinations of Fox and Berlin have predetermined for them the relative merit of the Marduka text before it is even considered.[75] Finally, the presence of some clearly-fictitious genres in the Bible suggests that question of historicity can be less important than the theological message of the narrative. If it is the case that Esther's theological message is not necessarily rooted

---

[68] Not listed here is the oft-cited, but seldom-accepted view of Shemaryahu Talmon, "'Wisdom' in the Book of Esther," *Vetus Testamentum* 13 no. 4 (1963): 419–455 that Esther is a historicized wisdom tale. See Kevin McGeough "Esther the Hero: Going Beyond 'Wisdom' in Heroic Narratives," *Catholic Biblical Quarterly* 70 no. 1 (2008): 44–65 for an evaluation of this approach to Esther through the lens of heroic narratives.

[69] E.g., Edward J. Young. *An Introduction to the Old Testament* (Grand Rapids: Zondervan, 1949), 375–377.

[70] Cf. Clines, *Ezra, Nehemiah, Esther,* 256–257 for a distinction between this view and the next.

[71] Moore, *Esther,* liii.

[72] Closely related to this is Robert Alter, *The Art of Biblical Narrative* (New York: Basic Books, 1981), 34, who calls it "a comic fantasy using pseudo-historical materials."

[73] Paton, *Esther,* 75–77.

[74] Weiland, "Historicity, Genre, and Narrative Design," 155. Cf. Dillard and Longman, 193.

[75] Firth, "The Third Quest," 240–241.

in its historical veracity—particularly if the narrator has clued the reader in to a genre other than historical narrative—then too much ink has been spilled debating a point that matters less than what the text means. While arguing for historicity is vital for some biblical matters (e.g., the Resurrection, cf. 1 Cor 15.12–19), it matters far less in others.[76] If the believer spends all of his or her energy debating the historical nature of the Esther narrative, but misses the lessons that can be learned, it matters very little whether or not he was right in his argument, for he has missed God's message.

## C. Conclusion

Aside from the historical question, which has recently occupied the primary place in Esther's interpretive history, the common question that seems to lie beneath most of the history of interpretation regarding Esther is whether or not it has any religious or moral value. Early translations and rabbinic retellings explicitly added morality to the narrative. Some expositors ignored it because of its lack of religion, while others despised it for the same reason. The entire question of canonicity seems to have been bound up in this same matter. The primary conundrum of Esther, then, is what to do with a biblical book that seems so unbiblical.

If, however, it can be shown from internal evidence, without any appeal to additions or strained exegesis, that the book of Esther has a religious undergirding, there will be less need to

---

[76] Another example of this may be precise nature of the days of creation, which matters far less than understanding that God created in six days to establish the theology of the Sabbath—a biblical theme that runs from the giving of the Law (Exod 20.8–11) through eternity (Heb 4.1–11). See Nathan Ward, *The Growth of the Seed: Notes on the Book of Genesis* (Chillicothe: DeWard Publishing, 2007), 39–40 for a further discussion of this interpretive issue.

give the story of Esther its own cosmetic enhancements to cover up the story's blemishes.[77] This issue will take center stage in the next part of this book.

---

[77] Dunne, *Esther and Her Elusive God*, 69. This is Dunne's description of what many expositors do with Esther to avoid the difficulties in the text.

# PART TWO

---

# God and Religion in Esther

# THREE

## *Religion in the Book of Esther*

The entirety of this section might seem like an odd issue to raise about a biblical book. But, as is often noted, God is not mentioned anywhere in the text of Esther, either by his name Yahweh (יהוה), the more generic "God" (אֱלֹהִים), or any of the other "El" (אֵל) variants. Jerusalem and the temple are never mentioned, nor are the Law or covenant, love or forgiveness. No one prays, prophesies, has a vision, or performs a miracle. On this basis, Jobes says, "If one went through the text and replaced every occurrence of the word 'Jews' with the name of some other ethnic group, there would be no reason to think the story had anything at all to do with the Bible."[1]

For this reason, the first step in building a case that Esther should be read in a providential context is to argue Esther should be read in a religious context. Further, that the history of interpretation so frequently adds religious elements and moralizes the characters suggests this is a key matter to examine. This discussion will consist of two parts: first, I will address the question of whether the characters in Esther are religious; second, I will explore whether, or to what extent, the author framed the narrative in a religious context. The first question, as we will see,

---

[1] Jobes, *Esther*, 19.

is harder to answer with any certainty and, ultimately, not all will agree. The second has a much clearer answer. Thus, in the following chapters, I will argue that, whether or not the characters in the narrative of Esther are exemplars of morality, the story itself is written in such a way as to be read in the context of the Old Testament canon.

There is little-to-no evidence from the narrative to suggest the characters see themselves as devotees of Yahweh. Instead, a reading that does not presume a Judeo-Christian point of view might suggest Esther and Mordecai have been fully assimilated into Persian culture. Dunne, for example, argues the characters in Esther are completely secular.[2] Further, he agrees with Klaassen that the Purim festival of drunkenness, parallel to the Persian feasting of Esther 1, "shows the extent to which the Jews have become Persian."[3]

The "morality" of the heroes also may call into question the religiousness of the story. While it is natural for the average Christian to view them in the best possible light because they are beloved Bible characters, another reading is a legitimate interpretive option. For example, they are Jews who chose not to return to the Promised Land.[4] Esther shows no concern for dietary laws when brought into the king's court, and she conceals her Jewish identity during the search for a queen and continues

---

[2] Dunne, *Esther and Her Elusive God*, 4.

[3] Ibid., 65.

[4] Ibid., 19. Dunne points to this as evidence of the assimilation that took place during the exile, contrasting it with Jeremiah 51.50 and Psalm 137.5–6. While Esther's apparent indifference to Jerusalem is a striking contrast with Nehemiah (Neh 1), the reader must be careful not to indict all Diaspora Jews of all time as secular and assimilated or to presume that we have full insight into Esther's mindset from the basis of this narrative alone.

to do so as queen.[5] She then loses her virginity in the bed of an uncircumcised pagan king to whom she is not married. She only risks her life by going to the king after Mordecai points out that she will not escape harm if she refuses to act. Finally, when she finds out the Jews have killed 500 people in Susa, she asks that the massacre be permitted for yet another day and the bodies of Haman's ten sons be impaled on the city gate.

Mordecai can also be seen in a less-than-positive light. He is the one who insists Esther conceal her Jewish identity, even though it would mean compromising whatever faith she has and violating the law. His refusal to pay homage to Haman is what jeopardizes the entire Jewish people and his motivation is unknown—that early interpreters added the element of idolatry shows their concern to clarify what was left vague in the text.[6] Some interpreters have even suggested his statement that Esther would not escape death was a thinly-veiled threat.[7]

The text does not reveal much about the motives and thoughts of Esther and Mordecai. The narrator does not say what Esther thought about being taken into the king's harem or why Mordecai refused to bow to Haman and neither exonerates nor

---

[5] Iain Duguid, "But Did They Live Happily Ever After? The Eschatology of the Book of Esther" *Westminster Theological Journal* 68 (2006): 89 points out she lived such an assimilated life that even her closest companions were unaware of her Jewishness, which likely meant ignoring essentially all of the Law.

[6] A variety of motives have been suggested for Mordecai's refusal to bow. In addition Haman expecting worship (or some other idolatrous interpretation), it has been suggested Mordecai was disgruntled over being passed over for the promotion Haman received or that Israelite-Amalekite conflict was the basis of the refusal. The only explanation the text gives is Mordecai's Jewishness (3.4). This is one of the key points where the narrator refuses entry into Mordecai's psyche. See Fox, *Character and Ideology*, 191–195.

[7] See Ronald W. Pierce, "The Politics of Esther and Mordecai," *Bulletin for Biblical Research* 2 (1992): 87, who argues Mordecai is prepared to kill Esther himself if she does not try to save her people.

condemns Esther and Mordecai nor evaluates their behavior as good or bad in the eyes of the Lord.[8] As a result, the reader is left to decide whether Esther and Mordecai should be viewed with rose-tinted lenses or to presume the worst as some interpreters have. The truth, as usual, is likely somewhere in the middle.[9] Even this, however, raises the question of the religiousness of the book: if the heroes of the story are not models of faith, how religious a story can it be?

As a result of such interpretive issues and problematic questions, many have taken a strong position against Esther. For example, as noted in chapter 1, Calvin never preached from Esther and did not include it among his commentaries. He is not the only one. Pfeiffer asserts that "secular nationalism" is the book's guiding light and that the author considered religion a garment to be lightly discarded whenever it hindered worldly aims.[10] Cornhill calls it "an entirely profane story in a purely worldly sense for the sake of satisfying worldly pleasures and instincts,"[11] and Bertheau says, "It stands further from the spirit of the Old Testament revelation and the Gospel than any other book in the Old Testament."[12]

---

[8] Jobes, *Esther*, 20.

[9] Dunne, *Esther and Her Elusive God*, 15–67 makes a compelling case for a fully assimilated and secularized reading of the characters, though he perhaps overstates his case in some instances. For example, after rightfully pointing out minute details that many expositors miss in certain texts, he ignores the fact that Mordecai's counter-edict is explicitly written as a self-defense measure, saying, "[T]he edict itself points toward the reversal of roles, the persecuted have become the persecutors" (63) (though Dunne's primary issue is with the second day of fighting [John Anthony Dunne, personal correspondence, July 3, 2015]).

[10] Robert Pfeiffer, *Introduction to the Old Testament* (New York: Harper & Bros., 1948), 742–743.

[11] C.H. Cornhill, *Einleitung in das Alte Testament* (Leipzig, 1891), 153.

[12] Qtd. in Bernhard W. Anderson, "The Place of the Book of Esther in the Christian Bible," *Journal of Religion* 30 (1950): 34.

Others are even more strongly against it. As mentioned previously, Luther is well known as expressing his hostility to Esther, wishing even that it did not exist as it "Judaize[s] too greatly and [has] much pagan rubbish." [13] Jewish scholar Samuel Sandmel echoes the sentiment: "I should not be grieved if the book of Esther were somehow dropped out of Scripture." [14] Pfeiffer goes on to say, "Such a secular book hardly deserves a place in the canon of Sacred Scriptures." [15] Eissfeldt says, "Christianity... has neither occasion nor justification for holding onto it," [16] and Morris calls it "a standing embarrassment to Christian expositors." [17] Anderson says, "One gains the impression that the author had an indifferent, if not cynical, attitude toward the Jewish religion. Not least of all, the book is inspired by a fierce nationalism and an unblushing vindictiveness which stand in glaring contradiction to the Sermon on the Mount. Surely this book is of the earth." [18] Anderson goes on to say it unveils the dark passions of the human heart—such as envy, hatred, fear, anger, vindictiveness, and pride—which are then blended into an intense nationalism. He ultimately concludes, "A more human book has never been written." [19]

---

[13] Martin Luther, *Table Talk,* 22.2080.

[14] Samuel Sandmel, *The Enjoyment of Scripture* (New York: Oxford, 1972), 44.

[15] Pfeiffer, *Introduction to the Old Testament,* 743.

[16] Otto Eissfeldt, *The Old Testament: An Introduction* (New York: Harper and Row, 1965), 511–512.

[17] A.E. Morris, "The Purpose of the Book of Esther," *Expository Times* 42 (1930–31): 128.

[18] Anderson, "Esther in the Christian Bible,"32.

[19] Ibid., 39. Bruce W. Jones, "Two Misconceptions about the Book of Esther," *Catholic Biblical Quarterly* 30 no. 2 (1977): 171–181 takes these approaches to task. After carefully working through various objections, he concludes, "Those who are offended by the blood and by the so-called Jewish nationalism are either literalists or are acting as if they

Morris, after celebrating "emancipation from the tyranny of verbal inspiration" in regard to Esther says, "As history it would be a serious blot upon the character of the Jews; as an historical romance it condemns only those who delight in its repellent features."[20] Cornhill concludes, "Valuable as this book is to us as a document for the history of religion, in receiving it into the collection of sacred writings the framers of the canon committed a serious blunder."[21] Finally, according to Anderson, "If a Christian minister is faithful to the context, he will not take his text from Esther; and, if the leader of a church-school class shows any Christian discernment, he will not waste time trying to show that the heroes of the book are models of character, integrity, and piety."[22] Fox, whose position has changed, said in an early article, "The lack of reference to God may show that [the author] did not intend his book to be regarded as sacred scripture."[23]

In addition to this modern distaste for Esther, the canonicity of Esther was debated for centuries. Among Jews, there seems to have been some hesitance to canonize a book "whose apparently vindictive spirit might be misunderstood by the Gentiles, and which instituted a festival for which they found no explicit sanction in the Law."[24] Even after it was acknowledged as canonical, discussion about its inspiration continued and its

---

were. Even when they recognize that the story is fiction, they treat it more seriously than it was intended. Pity the theologians who were offended because they could not laugh" (180–181).

[20] Morris, "Purpose of Esther," 124.

[21] Qtd. in Ibid., 124.

[22] Anderson, "Esther in the Christian Bible," 42.

[23] Fox, "The Religion of the Book of Esther," *Judaism* 39, no 2 (1990): 137. On Fox's changing position, see page 72n54 below.

[24] Anderson, "Esther in the Christian Bible," 32.

absence at Qumran—the only Old Testament book not found there—raises the question of how early Jews viewed it.

Christians also debated its canonicity. Esther was absent from the list of Bishop Melito of Sardis (AD 170).[25] Uncertainty about it is reflected in Christian catalogues as late as the fourth century as there was a strong tendency, especially among churches in the West, to view the book with suspicion.[26] Indeed, it is not quoted or even alluded to in the New Testament.[27]

But does Esther itself give any other indications it should be considered a religious work? The absence of everything associated with Israelite religion certainly seems to suggest it does not. Fox says, "If, then, we seek to interpret the author's intention, regarding that as the source and determinant of its primary (though not sole) meaning, we must try to read the book as an independent unit, unconstrained by the canonical contexts that it was later to enter."[28] This, however, begs the very question we are seeking to answer. While it may be true that a later placing of the book in a canonical context should not determine the nature of Esther, I will argue that it becomes apparent that the worldview of the author of Esther is fully congruent with the work's canonical location. This is most clear in a series of echoes of other Old Testament narratives that are interspersed throughout Esther and show it to be firmly within a canonical and religious context.[29]

---

[25] Eusebius, *Church History,* 4.26.13–14.

[26] Anderson, "Esther in the Christian Bible," 33.

[27] Brighton, "The Book of Esther," 204 says, "As far as the New Testament is concerned, Esther does not exist."

[28] Fox, "The Religion of the Book of Esther," 137.

[29] While the following study will engage with a variety of the interbiblical contexts, it does not exhaustively examine every aspect of all of them.

# FOUR

# Interbiblical Dialogue as a Clue to Esther's Religion

It has frequently been noted that the book of Esther alludes to other Old Testament narratives, though there has been debate as to which narrative it draws from. Gerleman suggests Esther should be read in the light of Exodus—taking clues from the foreign court, threat of death, deliverance, triumph, and establishment of a feast—and that Mordecai and Esther correspond to Moses and Aaron.[1] Many others, however, see a stronger connection with the Joseph story—taking clues from the foreign court, advancement from lowly status to high position, deliverance of people, and similar verbiage in certain passages.[2] Loader splits the difference, arguing it should be read as a new exodus story and as a new Joseph story.[3]

---

[1] Roland E. Murphy, *Wisdom Literature: Job, Proverbs, Ruth, Canticles, Ecclesiastes, and Esther.* The Forms of Old Testament Literature (Grand Rapids: Eerdmans, 1981), 154. Clines concludes Gerleman's claim is "too exclusive" *Ezra, Nehemiah, Esther,* 267.

[2] Sandra Berg, *The Book of Esther: Motifs, Themes and Structure,* SBL Dissertation Series 44 (Missoula: Scholars Press, 1979), 142, for example, investigates whether there is literary borrowing by the Esther author, concluding, "[T]he book of Esther seems dependent upon the story of Joseph, although the precise nature of, and reasons for, this dependence remain unclear."

[3] J.A. Loader, "Esther as a Novel with Different Levels of Meaning," *Zeitschrift für die Alttestamentliche Wissenschaft* 90 no. 3 (1978): 421.

The primary problem with an either/or approach to narrative influence is that it misses the multiplicity of echoes found throughout the Esther narrative from a variety of Hebrew Bible contexts. Allusions from all three sections of the Hebrew Canon frame the narrative of Esther in a canonical context.[4] While commentators often mention these echoes in passing, I am not aware of any who have undertaken a systematic compiling of these for the purpose of arguing the author intends his narrative to be understood within a religious framework.[5] The following section seeks to make such connections, thus showing that, regardless of whether the characters themselves are paragons of virtue, the context in which the author intended his story to be read was a religious one.[6]

## A. Mordecai and Saul
### (Est 2.5–9; 3.1; 9.10, 15–16, 22; 1 Sam 15.1–9)

Nearly all expositors of Esther have noted the strong connection between Mordecai and Saul. Mordecai is introduced

---

[4] It should be noted that this canonical context does not necessitate canonical inclusion. Esther's inclusion in the canon is a different matter entirely, which, while briefly discussed in chapter 2, is outside the scope of this book.

[5] The closest thing I have found to this are brief sections in the introductions of Laniak's, "Esther," 172–174 and David Firth, *The Message of Esther: God Present But Unseen*, The Bible Speaks Today (Downers Grove: Inter-Varsity Press, 2010), 33–35.

The issue of authorial intent is, admittedly, a hotly debated issue. It must be granted that, given the time, culture, and language differences (among other things), it can be difficult to determine an author's intent. Even so, some authors leave enough clues that the reader can reasonably infer what he or she had in mind while writing. This book will argue this is the case with Esther's author and his or her religious views.

[6] The following does not take into account every proposed connection, but only those which I feel are the strongest. For example, Jonathan Grossman, "'Dynamic Analogies' in the book of Esther," *Vetus Testamentum* 59 (2009): 394–414, offers plausible connections to the Jacob/Esau story, the Ahab/Jezebel/Naboth story, the greatness of Joshua, and even the building and inauguration of the temple.

as a Benjaminite descendant of Kish (Est 2.5)[7] and Haman as an Agagite (Est 3.1), thus immediately calling to mind the Benjaminite son of Kish, King Saul (1 Sam 9.1–2), and his conflict with Agag, king of Amalek (1 Sam 15.1–9). The battle with Agag was one of Saul's most detrimental failings (1 Sam 15.22–23, 26–29). Rather than fulfilling the Holy War God assigned him, Saul spared some of the Amalekites and took plunder, allegedly to offer sacrifices to God. In Esther, we have a conflict between a Kishite and an Agagite that again results in war. In this instance, the Jews utterly destroy their enemies and do not take any plunder (Est 9.5–19). As a result of these connections, some see Esther 9 in the context of Old Testament Holy War.[8] Another connection is that Israel's rest from her enemies is tied to the destruction of the Amalekites (Deut 25.19). In Esther, with this task completed, the Jews enjoy "rest from their enemies" (9.22).[9]

## B. Nabal and Amnon, Ahasuerus and Haman
### (Est 1.10; 5.9; 1 Sam 25.36; 2 Sam 13.28)

Ahasuerus makes his decision to invite Vashti to the party when "the heart of the king was merry with wine"

---

[7] Whether the Kish in Mordecai's genealogy is to be understood as identical with Saul's father is a debated matter that hinges some on the antecedent of אֲשֶׁר in Esther 2.6, who was taken captive with Jeconiah. The immediate antecedent is Kish, which would exclude the possibility of him also being Saul's father. The other option is Mordecai, though he seems far too young in the narrative to have been a deportee. An attractive solution suggested by Dunne, *Esther and Her Elusive God,* 20n5 is that Mordecai is the antecedent, but the text is not indicating they are contemporaries but instead expressing "corporate solidarity in exile." At the very least, the narrator surely expects the reader to make this connection, especially when the thrice repeated refrain about not taking plunder (9.10, 15, 16) is added.

[8] See page 106 below for more on Holy War in Esther.

[9] Dillard and Longman, *An Introduction to the Old Testament,* 197.

(כְּטוֹב לֵב־הַמֶּלֶךְ בַּיָּיִן). Haman, after drinking to celebrate his plan
(3.15) and revel in his honor (5.6), was "glad of heart" (וְטוֹב לֵב
5.9). With the Samuel connection already established, it is striking that only two other individuals are said to have merry hearts
from the consumption of alcohol: Nabal, who resisted David
(1 Sam 25.36), and Amnon, who raped Tamar (2 Sam 13.28),
both of whom made foolish decisions that led to their downfall.[10]
Likewise, in the Esther narrative, the wine-filled glad heart led
to decisions that were the undoing of Ahasuerus and Haman.
With Ahasuerus, his decision to parade his wife before the men
of the party was rebuffed, and he was left with what he perceived to be a major state crisis—one that ultimately led to the
publicity of his shame by royal edict and his choice of a wife
who was more domineering. Haman's downfall was even more
dramatic. His glad heart led him to listen to his wife's advice (in
violation of Ahasuerus' decree!) and seek the execution of Mordecai—only to be compelled to honor Mordecai and die on the
very stake he prepared for Mordecai.

## C. Esther and Daniel
### (Est 2.8–10; Dan 1.8–16)

Many commentators have noted the similarities between Esther and Daniel at the beginning of each book. Each account
begins with a young Jew in a foreign court with emphasis placed
on Jewishness, food, and relationship. Daniel refuses the food
because of his Jewishness (Dan 1.8);[11] Esther hides her Jewish-

---

[10] David G. Firth, "When Samuel Met Esther: Narrative Focalisation, Intertextuality, and Theology," *Southeastern Theological Review* 1 no. 1 (2010): 23.

[11] Joyce Baldwin, *Daniel: An Introduction and Commentary,* Tyndale Old Testament
Commentaries (Downers Grove: Intervarsity Press, 1978), 83 argues Daniel's motivation
for not eating was not kosher laws, which do not require a diet of vegetables and water,

ness and accepts the food (Est 2.9–10), apparently having "no ethical qualms about eating the empire's food and being used as the emperor's plaything."[12] This particular echo may be intended to convey the moral weakness of the main characters as the story begins.[13]

## D. Mordecai and Joseph
### (Est 3.2–5; Gen 39.6b–10)[14]

After alerting King Ahasuerus to a plot against his life, Mordecai is passed over for a promotion that is instead given to Haman (Est 2.19–3.1). Upon his appointment, the King issues a decree that everyone bow to Haman, a law Mordecai refuses to honor (Est 3.2). Joseph, a slave in Egypt, has been appointed to

---

but that sharing a meal was to commit oneself to friendship, covenant relationship, and dependence.

[12] Iain Duguid, *Esther and Ruth*, Reformed Expository Commentary, (Phillipsburg: P&R Publishing, 2005), 23. He continues, "At this point in the story, Esther is certainly no Daniel. She is both in the world *and* of the world, fully complying with the empire's outrageous demands with the goal of winning the 'love' of an unworthy royal husband. She would perhaps have objected that she had little choice, but if someone is willing to suffer the consequences, full obedience to God's law is always an option. Vashti, the pagan, had already shown in the previous chapter that the empire cannot ultimately compel our obedience" (29).

[13] An alternate, though less likely, explanation is that their different circumstances required different reactions (cf. Baldwin, *Esther*, 67).

[14] Some have sought to connect this scene to the story in Daniel 3 (see Carol Bechtel, *Esther*, Interpretation [Louisville: John Knox Press, 2002], 37 and Duguid, *Esther and Ruth*, 34–35 as well as chapter 1 for additions that reflect this perspective) as an explanation of why Mordecai did not bow, viz. he would only bow to God. Although some argue that Haman would have expected a worshipful bow (e.g., Breneman, *Ezra, Nehemiah, Esther*, 327: "Persians saw it as an act of reverence that bordered on recognizing the official as divine"; cf. Keil, "Esther," 213–214, who makes the case from Herodotus), Dunne, *Esther and Her Elusive God*, 36–37 argues that Mordecai would have had to show such deference to the king on multiple occasions in order to have attained his current position (cf. Huey, "Esther," 812) and many commentators point to Esther's later falling down before the king in Esther 8 (e.g., Duguid, *Esther and Ruth*, 33). In short, it is doubtful that Mordecai's motivation stemmed from anything as noble as refusing to worship Haman.

a significant position within Potiphar's house when the mistress of the house begins to desire him (Gen 39.7). Both Mordecai and Joseph are appealed to "day by day" (יוֹם וָיוֹם), but "would not listen" (וְלֹא־שָׁמַע) (Gen 39.10; Est 3.4). As a result, both situations result in angry false accusations that place a previously-trusted Jewish exile in danger of death (Gen 39.13–18; Est 3.8–9). Potiphar's wife lied that Joseph tried to rape her. Haman engaged in a series of truths, half-truths, and lies to accomplish his purposes of convincing Ahasuerus to sign off on his edict. The statement that the Jews' laws are different from everyone else is true, but slanted with a falsely negative connotation. The statement that they do not follow the king's laws is false—only one Jew refused to follow one law. Finally, that it does not profit the king to tolerate such a people is patently false, since the Jew in question saved the king's life in the previous chapter.[15] However, against all odds, both of these endangered Jews become agents of Jewish salvation and are promoted to higher positions, made second only to the king.[16] Such a strong resonance with the Joseph story, particularly in the motifs of danger and elevation, could be intended to be a hint at God's providential actions in the story of Esther.

## E. Esther, Jonah, and Joel
### (Est 4.3, 14; Jon 3.9; Joel 2.12, 14)

There are strong verbal parallels in these passages. Esther 4.3 and Joel 2.12 both have "fasting" (צוֹם), "weeping" (בְכִי), and "lamenting" (מִסְפֵּד) in the same order, and Jonah 3.9 also speaks of widespread fasting in "sackcloth and ashes" (שַׂק וָאֵפֶר). Final-

---

[15] See J.G. McConville, *Ezra, Nehemiah, and Esther,* The Daily Study Bible Series (Philadelphia: The Westminster Press, 1985), 167.

[16] Levenson, *Esther,* 68.

ly, along with Esther 4.14, Joel 2.14 and Jonah 3.9 ask, "Who knows?" (מִי יוֹדֵעַ), all of which show the same perspective of faith in God's action without presuming to know what he will do.[17] The Jonah story also features the reversal of an irreversible edict of destruction (Jon 3.10).[18]

### F. Moses and Esther
#### (Est 4–5; Exod 1–15)

A full summation of all of the connections in these chapters between Esther and the story of Moses is beyond the purview of this subsection. In brief, both Moses and Esther received privileges of nobility without being born into it. Both gave up the comforts of their unusual positions to identify with their people instead of those with whom they resided, which involved interceding before the king. Both are hesitant: Esther considers remaining silent and Moses argues to God that he cannot speak eloquently. Both have a life-threatening encounter. The success of each is connected with finding "favor" (חֵן). Ultimately, both risk this favored status by returning to the court of the Gentile king to seek the deliverance of their people. Finally, both stories have a connection to Passover.[19]

### G. Haman and Joseph
#### (Est 6.6–10; Gen 41.39–45)

The echo here is one of contrast between the honors bestowed upon Joseph at his ascension to the position of grand vizier and

---

[17] See Jobes, *Esther*, 137 and Laniak, "Esther," 230 for the Esther/Joel connection. See chapter 9 of this book for a further discussion of the "who knows?" question within the context of modern ministry.

[18] Laniak, "Esther," 229.

[19] Ibid., 229–230. On the Passover connection specifically, see pages 64–65 below.

Haman's private desires for his own glory.[20] At each point of Haman's request, Haman seeks more than the usual level of honor. Whereas Joseph receives a linen garment and gold necklace (Gen 41.42), Haman sought a garment the king himself had worn (Est 6.8). Joseph rides in the chariot of the second in command (Gen 41.43); Haman wants to ride on the king's own steed, dressed in royal array (Est 6.8).[21] A simple call of "bow the knee" precedes Joseph as he is honored by the people (Gen 41.43); Haman wants it declared that the king himself honors him (Est 6.9).[22] Laniak concludes Haman wants to be honored *like* a king *by* the king, that he has royal ambitions that are at the expense of true loyalty to the king; "In contrast, Mordecai and Joseph … are presented as paragons of loyalty to their sovereigns."[23] Among other things, this scene reveals something about Haman's character: it is not that his great ambition is to play dress-up, but that he desires to be king.[24] As Bechtel points out, with Ahasuerus' signet ring, adding the king's clothes and horse "would represent a virtual clean sweep. The only 'thing' Haman would lack would be the queen."[25]

---

[20] The difference between Egyptian and Persian culture, not to mention the amount of time that has passed between Joseph and Esther, may account for some of the differences. On the other hand, some things would have been seen as overreaching in any cultural context of any era (e.g., wearing the king's clothes and riding the king's horse). Beyond that, the strong series of parallels between Joseph's story and Esther's invites the reader to make the comparison between the two scenes.

[21] See page 161 below for comment on the "royal crown" as it relates to the horse.

[22] Clines, *Ezra, Nehemiah, Esther,* 308. Cf. Laniak, "Esther," 241.

[23] Laniak, "Esther," 242.

[24] Ibid. also says that he is likely "seeking royal validation for succession to the throne."

[25] Bechtel, *Esther,* 59. Perhaps, for all the buffoonery of King Ahasuerus (see pages 81–84 below), he is not so daft as to miss the significance of Haman's request. It may be his reaction to Haman's falling on Esther's couch in 7.7–9 is prompted by this very conversation—either because he mistook it for a sexual assault to lay claim to the

## H. Purim and Passover

(Est 3.7, 12; 4.1, 12; Exod 12.1–28; cf. Lev 23.4–8)

One of the purposes of Esther is to provide the etiology of the feast of Purim,[26] the one Jewish feast which has no commendation in the Law of Moses. The Exodus connections alone, mentioned above, make a parallel between Purim and Passover attractive. Such a link is virtually impossible to miss when it is realized that Haman's edict is written on Nisan 13, mere hours before the Passover feast would begin.[27] From there, the story becomes one of threat and deliverance featuring a Jew with unlikely royal connections and a precedent-setting ritual, with formal legislation regarding the perpetual festival observation to follow.[28]

In addition to this, Webb connects both Passover and Purim with the Abrahamic promise, because of the Agag/Kish connection. This link marks the conflict in Esther as merely the

---

throne or because he saw it as a convenient excuse to execute a person with known royal aspirations.

Some have also suggested Ahasuerus' jealousy may have been aroused by Haman repeatedly being invited to the banquets. McConville, *Ezra, Nehemiah, and Esther,* 177 points out that although the first dinner is "for the king" (5.4), the second is "for the king and Haman" (5.8): "There is just a hint here that Esther's purpose is to sow a resentment in the king's mind and have him think that this Haman was staking too big a claim both in the kingdom and in his wife's esteem" (cf. Ze'ev Weisman, *Political Satire in the Bible* [Atlanta: Scholars Press, 1998], 151).

[26] Paton, *Esther,* 55–56 sees it as the "one purpose from beginning to end," though few others have agreed it is so exclusive in its focus (but see Howard, *Old Testament Historical Books,* 330–331).

[27] Esther's fast should also be considered in the context of Passover. Does the fast mean the situation is so severe they fast on Passover itself (Clines, *Ezra, Nehemiah, Esther,* 303) or that they are so secularized they are not showing trust in God at the very moment when the need for it should be most obvious (Dunne, *Esther and Her Elusive God,* 55)? One's answer to this question will certainly be determined by his or her view of the characters in the narrative.

[28] Laniak, "Esther," 262. Cf. Hamilton, *Handbook on the Historical Books,* 545 for more connections.

next chapter in an ongoing conflict, which began when the Amalekites tried to destroy Israel after the Exodus (Exod 17.8), which was itself rooted in the promises to Abraham, Isaac, and Jacob (Exod 2.24).[29] Because of this connection, Webb argues that Purim and Passover, "standing back to back in the festival cycle, testify to two complementary aspects of a single reality: the election of Israel, which had its beginning historically in the call of Abraham."[30]

## I. Purim and Zion
### (Est 9.22; Jer 31.13)

Jeremiah 30–34 is one of the few prolonged bright spots in an otherwise dismal book. Among other things, these chapters contain Jeremiah's vision of the exiles returning to Zion, where God will "turn their mourning into joy ... and give them gladness for sorrow" (Jer 31.13). In the very verse that connects the Jews' victory over their enemies with God's promise of rest in Deuteronomy, we read of "the month that had been turned for them from sorrow into gladness and from mourning into a holiday" (Est 9.22). The verbal connection between these two passages is strong, as each passage uses "turned" (הָפַךְ), "sorrow" (יָגוֹן), "mourning" (אֵבֶל), and "gladness" (שָׂמַח).[31] According to

---

[29] Webb, *Five Festal Garments*, 127.

[30] Ibid., 128. Weiland, "Literary Clues to God's Providence in the Book of Esther," *Bibliotheca Sacra* 160 (2003): 45–46 argues that Haman's plot "struck at the heart of the Abrahamic covenant," since his intention would have annulled the promises made to Abraham and his offspring, including the Messianic line and God's plan to bring salvation to both Jews and Gentiles. He says, "Whereas disobedience to the Mosaic Law brought about the covenant curse of captivity, the promises of the Abrahamic Covenant assured that the Jews would not be eradicated as a people and God's purposes could not be ultimately thwarted."

[31] On gladness, Jeremiah uses the verb; Esther uses the noun (שִׂמְחָה).

Laniak, the use of these terms frames this event "in terms of God's covenant faithfulness to the postexilic community." [32] If this is correct, then it places the Esther story squarely in the context of God's covenant relationship with Israel. [33]

## J. Esther and Christ

(Est 3.7, 12; 4.16; 5.1; 8.17; Matt 26–28 and parallels) [34]

Some authors find Christ in every chapter of Esther, [35] while others eschew any connection between the two. [36] As I will show, while Beckett and Wells certainly go too far in some of their allegorizing, Dunne's approach is too extreme. If it can be

---

[32] Laniak, "Esther," 263.

[33] The implications of this covenant relationship is debated. Although it could be argued that this connection vindicates Diaspora Judaism (cf. Jobes, *Esther*, 42), Huey, "Esther," 787 and Dunne, *Esther and Her Elusive God*, 4–5 both argue God's conspicuous absence in the narrative shows God is faithful and steadfast even though the people do not deserve it. In "Irony as the Key to Understanding the Book of Esther," *Southwestern Journal of Theology* 32 no. 3 (1990): 38–39, Huey goes even further, arguing the primary intent of the book is "to show that the post-exilic people of Israel have not changed in spite of the punishment inflicted on them" and that God's hiddenness may indicate his disapproval of their acts. Huey concludes that instead of providence being the key to understanding the book, just the opposite may be the intent: "[B]ecause his people did not seek help from God, he deliberately became the hidden God." Similarly, Elsie R. Stern, "Esther and the Politics of Diaspora" *The Jewish Quarterly Review* 100 no. 1 (2010): 25–53 argues Esther does not defend diaspora life, but comically critiques it.

[34] Messianic foreshadowing is, admittedly, a difference in kind rather than degree from Old Testament interbiblical dialog. Among other things, this is not just a canonical reading that goes in both directions, but a diachronic development of innerbiblical echoes that accumulate through Scripture. (Thanks to Tim Laniak for helping to clarify this distinction.) Its discussion is included here for the sake of convenience.

[35] See, e.g., Michael Beckett, *Gospel in Esther* (Carlisle: Paternoster Press, 2002) or Samuel Wells, "Esther," *Esther and Daniel*, Brazos Theological Commentary on the Bible (Grand Rapids: Brazos Press, 2013) for some of the more thoroughgoing Christological approaches.

[36] Dunne, *Esther and Her Elusive God*, 120 writes, "In our attempt to situate Esther within a broader theological framework we must avoid a major pitfall. I have in mind the attempt to turn Esther into an allegory for the church."

reasonably presumed that what was argued in chapter 2 about the canon in Jesus' day is accurate,[37] then Jesus' teaching about himself from all the Old Testament (Luke 24.27) and his statement that all Scripture refers to him (Luke 24.44) must mean *something* in the context of the Esther scroll.[38]

The connection is stronger than might be first expected. The life-and-death struggle for both Esther and Christ begins at Passover, which is immediately followed by Esther's fast and Christ's humiliation. Wechsler connects these two, arguing the "fast" in Scripture is usually associated with the idea of affliction or humiliation. He says that in Mishnaic and later Hebrew, צום ("fast") and חענית ("humiliation") are used synonymously, and that in the LXX, the idea of "afflicting one's soul" is often a euphemism for fasting.[39] According to Collins, these trappings of fasting (e.g., sackcloth, torn clothes, ashes) "represented the symbolic contact of the mourner with death,"[40] causing Wechsler to conclude the three-day fast may be understood as foreshadowing the three-day death of Christ.[41]

This connection between the fast of Esther and the death of Christ is strengthened by the fast ending on the third day.

---

[37] See page 30, above.

[38] Admittedly, the merits of this argument depend upon one's view of Jesus, Inspiration, and other such theological matters.

[39] Michael G. Wechsler, "Shadow and Fulfillment in the Book of Esther," *Bibliotheca Sacra* 154 (1997): 281.

[40] Nina L. Collins, "Did Esther Fast on the 15th Nisan? An Extended Comment on Esther 3.12," *Revue Biblique* 100 (1993): 535n10.

[41] Wechsler, "Shadow and Fulfillment," 282. An irony that arises here is that the LXX regards Haman's death as by crucifixion, which made Haman, for many Jews, the best known victim of crucifixion. The annual Purim reading of Esther, where Jews would rejoice in the crucifixion and mocking of Haman could very easily lead to the same regarding Jesus. See T.C.G. Thornton, "The Crucifixion of Haman and the Scandal of the Cross," *Journal of Theological Studies* 37 no. 2 (1986): 419–423.

In Paul's resurrection creed of 1 Corinthians 15, he says Christ was raised on the third day "in accordance with the Scriptures" (v 4). The difficulty interpreters face with this verse is there is no specific prophecy about a third day resurrection—a matter handled differently by various exegetes.[42] One possibility is represented by those who have pointed to "a slew of texts that link 'the third day' with the day of salvation and divine manifestation."[43] If Paul does refer to the Old Testament tradition of third day salvation, then Esther's appearance before Ahasuerus to plead for the Jewish people could be seen in this Christological light. Further, Esther exchanging her garments of humiliation for garments of royalty (LXX: "glorious attire") before approaching the king to intercede for her people may also be typologically connected with Christ's being "crowned with glory and honor" (Heb 2.9; cf. Acts 3.13; Phil 2.8–9; 1 Pet 1.21) and intercessory work.[44] Finally, as a result of the decree that will result from Esther's intercessory work, "many from the peoples of the country declared themselves Jews" (Est 8.17). While the precise nature of this conversion is debated and is outside the scope of this book, within this context, it parallels the salvific work of Christ: "[T]he salvation occasioned by the presentation of Jesus resulted in the inclusion of Gentiles into the community of those who worship Yahweh."[45]

---

[42] See Gordon Fee, *The First Epistle to the Corinthians,* The New International Commentary on the New Testament (Grand Rapids: Eerdmans, 1987), 726–728 for an enumeration and brief discussion of various interpretive options.

[43] David E. Garland, *1 Corinthians,* Baker Exegetical Commentary on the New Testament (Grand Rapids: Baker Academic, 2003), 687. Cf. Craig L Blomberg, *1 Corinthians,* The NIV Application Commentary (Grand Rapids: Zondervan, 1994), 296.

[44] Wechsler, "Shadow and Fulfillment," 283.

[45] Ibid. Cf. Hebrews 7.25; Galatians 3.8, 28–29; et al.

In addition to the connection between Esther's fast and the Passion is the final solution in Esther 10. After the Jews' great victories and the subsequent edicts about Purim, life returns to normal in the Persian Empire—Ahasuerus taxes the people and Mordecai goes about his business, rising in favor with the populace (10.1–3). All seems well. The problem with this ending, however, is that no Jewish reader could have possibly seen a Benjaminite descendant of Kish, second to a pagan emperor, as God's grand solution. Duguid asks, "How could anyone possibly remember the receiving of rest from one's enemies without thinking about God, and more specifically about God's promise to David of rest for Israel and peace while they dwelt in their own land?"[46] While it is certainly better for Mordecai to occupy the position of grand vizier than for Haman to do so, it is anticlimactic in the larger canonical context, the very context in which the book of Esther is so firmly set. Further, as long as an emperor who is indifferent to genocide remains on the throne, the danger has not fully passed.

Duguid concludes,

> It was good news that Mordecai was now second in rank to Xerxes, in a place where he was able to seek good for his people and speak peace to all his seed (Est 10.3). The position once filled by the enemy of the Jews was now occupied by their friend. This was good news, but it was not yet the best of news. A major crisis had been resolved but the consummation had not yet occurred. When they truly had rest from their enemies all around, their king would surely no longer be named Xerxes, but would be a king who embodies the virtues described in Psalm 72, especially the pursuit of justice and righteousness. True rest would come when the one who seeks their good and speaks their peace was not a descendant

---

[46] Duguid, "Eschatology," 95.

of Saul who was *second in rank* to anyone but the promised seed of David, reigning as the true king.

In other words, the text itself shows us that the great reversal of the Book of Esther is not yet the Great Reversal of all of history. It was not yet the inbreaking of the heavenly kingdom on earth. It was a great deliverance to be sure, a mighty victory of God against the kingdoms of this world, but any deliverance that rests on the influence of a single individual who must inevitably grow old and die, in an empire that has not been radically transformed, was at best only partial and temporary. The Book of Esther demonstrates the need for a greater reversal yet, one which would result in the coming of the true king, the Prince of Peace, whose reign will never end![47]

Thus, the solution in Esther points forward to something even greater: the coming Son of David who will rule, second to none, eternally, on God's very throne. Taken together, these connections to Christ, if deemed legitimate, place the story of Esther within the larger context of the biblical story of the coming Messiah.

## K. Minor Echoes

Once these larger connections have been established, other minor echoes can also be considered as at least potentially intentional. For example, according to Phillips, Esther 6.13 fits the pattern of non-Israelites aware of God's support for Israel (cf. Num 22–24; Josh 2.8–11; 1 Sam 4.8).[48] Similar to that is the familiar motif of the fear of God's people by the nations in 9.2 (see Exod 15.14–16; Ps 105.38).[49] Finally, Esther 9.30 contains

---

[47] Ibid., 95–96.

[48] Elaine Phillips, "Esther," *1 Chronicles–Job*, The Expositor's Bible Commentary (Grand Rapids: Zondervan, 2010), 647. Though, of course, God is not specifically mentioned by Zeresh.

[49] Levenson, *Esther*, 120. Cf. Phillips, "Esther," 662.

echoes of Zechariah 8.19, "which indicates that institutional-
ized fasts would become festivals of joy and urges the people of
God to love truth and peace." [50] While these are hardly strong
enough connections to build a case on when taken by themselves, the minor echoes add to an already substantial argument.

## L. Summary Observations

Not all of the echoes listed above are equally convincing, so
any single instance of such a connection could be written off
as either interpretive overreading or a mere coincidence. The
constant echoing of other Old Testament narratives, however,
cannot be ignored. Even if the minor echoes are disqualified
from consideration, the book of Esther still calls attention to
the books of Genesis, Deuteronomy, Samuel, Jonah, Jeremiah,
and Daniel, and points forward to the Gospels. It alludes to
the Abrahamic promise, Passover, Zion's Restoration, the long-
standing Amalekite conflict, and the Messiah. Whatever one
concludes about the religious leanings—or lack thereof—of
the principal characters in Esther, it is clear the author framed
his book within the context of the Israelite faith. Laniak, who
lists even more connections to the Joseph and Moses narratives,
rightly says,

> The author of Esther employs many conventions, themes, motifs,
> and terms borrowed from other stories in the Hebrew Bible. Es-
> ther is a thoroughly 'biblical' book in this sense. In its *intertextu-
> ality*, it provides an *interbiblical* dialog, making allusions to other
> heroes and incidents throughout. The naming of God in these
> other stories makes his presence all the more implicit in Esther.[51]

---

[50] Phillips, "Esther," 672.

[51] Laniak, "Esther," 172–173. In addition to Laniak's listing, see Gerleman and Berg

There are, to be sure, silences in Esther where the reader might prefer explicit statements. Given the "interbiblical dialog" in Esther, however, these blank spaces must be related to Scripture as a whole.[52] Firth also makes this point:

> Once we realise that so much of the story is told in a way that alludes to other passages in the Old Testament we begin to realise that our reading of Esther is meant to be shaped by what we know from these other passages and these allusions are consistently theological in their emphases. ... We are not seeking God in a text where he is absent. Rather, we are having our understanding of God enriched by the conversation that is generated.[53]

As Fox says, "Meaning depends on context, and, in the context of the canon, both Jewish and Christian, the Scroll is part of a larger testimony to God's control of history."[54] The interbiblical context provided by the author may help answer some of the questions about various verses in the narrative by directing our understanding of them to be providential. For example, much has been made of what Mordecai had in mind when he said deliverance would come from "another place" (Est 4.14),[55] but it could be argued that, to the modern reader,

---

for more exhaustive discussions of the Moses and Joseph connections, respectively.

[52] Jochen Teuffel, "Fate and Word: The Book of Esther as Guidance to a Canonical Reading of Scripture," *Currents in Theology and Mission* 36, no 1 (2009): 29–30.

[53] Firth, *The Message of Esther*, 34.

[54] "The Religion of the Book of Esther," 137. Fox's view of the religion of Esther is a moving target. In an earlier study (1980), he argues the theology of Esther is implied in the reversals ("The Religion of the Book of Esther," 142n30). In this article (1990), he concludes it is ultimately unknowable (145–147; cf. Fox, *Character and Ideology*, 246–247).

[55] The LXX, Targumim (Midr. *Leqah Tob* 4.14), and Josephus (*Ant.* 11.227, 279–282) all understand "place" to be an oblique reference to God, as it was used in later Jewish literature as a stand-in for God's name (cf. Talmon, "'Wisdom' in the Book of

Mordecai's meaning is less significant than the author's meaning. Even if one reads Mordecai as irreligiously as Dunne does,[56] the author may be hinting at the providential answer after all.[57] The New Testament clearly establishes the principle that people need not have full awareness of either the details of the prophecy or that they were even prophesying to speak prophetically. Peter tells his readers that the prophets who intended to speak for God did not fully understand their messages (1 Pet 1.10–12). More significantly, John tells us that Caiaphas,

---

Esther," 429n1, who suggests it is a substitute for the divine name and Moore, *Esther,* 50 who connects it to *eleos* in 1 Macc 16.3 and interprets it as "a veiled allusion to God.").

Others, such as Clines *Ezra, Nehemiah, and Esther,* 302, suggest it is not God ("deliverance through Esther and deliverance from God cannot be contrasted; and if 'place' means 'God,' who does '*another* place' mean…?"; cf. Howard, 323–324), but that it could be "Jewish officials (of similar standing to Nehemiah) or an armed revolt by the Jews." Firth, *The Message of Esther,* 76, suggests that it could refer to political deliverance, "so Mordecai might mean somewhere else, like Greece."

John Wiebe, "Will Relief and Deliverance Arise for the Jews from Another Place?" *Catholic Biblical Quarterly* 53 no. 3 (1991): 413, followed by Bush, *Ruth, Esther,* 395–397, Phillips, "Esther," 634–635, and Dunne, *Esther and Her Elusive God,* 44–46, suggests it be read "as an interrogative apodasis, asking in effect a rhetorical question expecting a negative answer." The effect of this is that Mordecai is telling Esther she is the only hope of salvation to the Jewish people: "He has no reason to expect it from any other place. He is attempting to motivate her to act." As Phillips, "Esther," 635 notes, this punctuation of the verse solves many of the difficulties that come with a traditional interpretation (e.g., from what other place would this deliverance come? why would they save Esther and her family if they did arrive?, etc.).

[56] Dunne follows Wiebe's rendering of 4.14b as a rhetorical question expecting a negative answer, concluding, "Mordecai is suggesting Esther is the only hope for the Jews; he is not expressing faith in God's sovereignty here. If Esther keeps silent, all the Jews will die. Period. … Mordecai does not assert confidence in God's providence here, but rather displays the opposite. Esther is the only hope, and there is nothing to suggest that Mordecai has any belief that God may indeed act to overcome the Jewish plight" (*Esther and Her Elusive God,* 46–47).

[57] Even if Wiebe's view is correct, given the interbiblical dialog taking place in Esther, what sounds like a negative rhetorical question to Esther surely sounds like a positive rhetorical question to the Jewish or Christian reader!

who did not intend to speak for God at all, prophesied unwittingly about Christ's death (John 11.49–53).

A second example of a potentially providential passage comes
from Mordecai's letter, recording the events that had transpired
leading up to the inauguration of the Feast of Purim. Mordecai
writes, "For Haman the Agagite, the son of Hammedatha, the
enemy of the Jews, had plotted against the Jews to destroy them,
and had cast Pur (that is, cast lots), to crush and to destroy them.
But when it[58] came before the king, he gave orders in writing
that his evil plan that he had devised against the Jews should
return on his own head, and that he and his sons should be
hanged on the gallows" (Est 9.24–25).

The difficulty with this passage is that it does not very closely
correspond to the events the book of Esther previously recorded.
In Esther 3, the king was complicit, if negligent, in signing the
death sentence of the Jewish people. In Esther 7, Harbona, one
of the king's eunuchs, suggests hanging Haman on the very gallows he built for Mordecai. In Esther 8, having executed Haman, Ahasuerus seemed initially reticent to doing anything
further,[59] yet eventually allows Esther and Mordecai to compose

---

[58] The pronoun is feminine and could refer to either Esther (e.g., RSV: "when Esther
came before the king") or the plot (e.g., NIV: "when the plot came to the king's attention"). Baldwin, *Esther*, 108–109 rightly suggests Mordecai's purpose is not to emphasize
his or Esther's role but to credit the king (but see Moore, *Esther*, 92–94 for an argument
from textual corruption that it refers to Esther).

[59] Ahasuerus reaction to Esther's request shows his primary concern was not to Haman's threat of Esther as a Jewess, but to Haman's threat of Esther as Ahasuerus' queen.
Bush, 445 says, "This understanding fits far better with the narrator's consistent characterization of the king as callously interested in little other than his own honor and power.
It seems far more likely [than him expressing a favorable disposition] that he is no more
concerned to be personally involved with the difficult task of saving this people from Haman's irrevocable degree than he was about their circumstances or identity when he gave
Haman permission for the odious decree to be issued in the first place."
Likewise, Timothy K. Laniak, *Shame and Honor in the Book of Esther*, SBL Dis-

a counter-decree. In chapter 9, Esther requests Haman's sons be hanged. Now, in Mordecai's record of what happens, Ahasuerus takes center stage: he learns of the plot; he hangs Haman; he gives orders that a counter-decree be written; and he orders that Haman's sons be hanged. Duguid suggests the mismatch between the letter and the events points to a king other than Ahasuerus who was truly in control of the events and changed the course of history to save the Jews. He argues that Ahasuerus is nowhere named because it was God himself who had reversed the fortunes of Haman and the Jews: "His decrees, written in the heavenly scrolls, were the only ones that truly could not be reversed!"[60] Duguid seems to suggest Mordecai did this intentionally, which is a more difficult position to prove. If, however, Mordecai is allowed to speak more truly than he knows, like Caiaphas after him, Mordecai's edict may hint strongly toward the inclusion of God.

Finally, the introduction of Mordecai and Esther (2.4–5) may offer a hint toward providence in the story. The shift from narrative to character introduction, smoothed over by most English translations, is abrupt. Midrash Esther Rabbah looks at a series of parallel passages (Exod 2.25; Jdg 4.4; 11.1; 1 Sam 17.12) where each abrupt introduction brought a new character who was the appropriate person for the task mentioned in the previous verse.[61] Thus, at the right moment, the right person was in the right place. What might initially ap-

---

sertation Series 165 (Atlanta: Scholars Press, 1998), 114 suggests Esther's accusation is rooted in their personal relationship, not his governance as a righteous king: "Esther has insinuated that the threat on her life is one directed at her *as his wife*. Framed this way, her words are, at the very least, a challenge to Ahasuerus *as a man*."

[60] Duguid, "Eschatology," 94.

[61] Midrash Esther Rabbah, 35.1. Cf. Beal, "Esther," 24.

pear to be merely coincidental must instead be understood as providential,[62] given the clear religious context in which the author has framed his narrative.

---

[62] See chapter 7 below on coincidence and providence.

FIVE

---

# *Literary Clues to God's Providence in Esther*

The author of Esther, I have argued, frames his narrative in an interbiblical, canonical context, which can, and likely should, suggest God is behind the scenes in the book of Esther. Another way the author accomplishes this is through a variety of literary features that point away from the human characters in the narrative.

## A. Irony

"Literary irony" refers to a reversal of fortune where actions and situations result in an outcome that is incongruous with what was expected.[1] As many scholars have noted, the book of Esther is filled with such irony.

### 1. Ahasuerus and Vashti

For example, in Esther 1, Ahasuerus summons Vashti to appear before the men at his stag party in her royal crown;[2] she refuses

---

[1] There are different types of irony. *Verbal irony* is the use of words to convey a meaning that is opposite to its literal meaning. *Dramatic irony* occurs when, in a narrative, the audience is aware of something the characters are not (e.g., Ahasuerus' and Haman's conversation in Esther 6). *Situational irony* is the irony under consideration here. Stan Goldman, "Narrative and Ethical Ironies in Esther," *Journal for the Study of the Old Testament* 47 (1990): 15–31 considers irony in different categories: *rhetorical* (textual), *generative* (interpretive; the reader's ethical response), or *intuitive* (authorial).

[2] The midrashim suggest the king requested she appear *only* in her royal crown, Cohen, *Megalith Esther*, 15, though this view is nearly universally rejected.

(1.10–12). As a result, the men of the empire overreact[3]—"She has wronged all the men of the empire and all women will now look at their husbands with contempt!" (1.16–17)—so Ahasuerus bans her from his presence and sends letters throughout the empire that all women must honor their husbands and every man must be the master in his own household (1.19–22).

That is, rather than using his unmitigated power to compel Vashti's obedience, he writes an irrevocable law that means she can never again come before the king; in essence, he officially sanctions her refusal to appear![4] Then, because of his great concern that women throughout the empire will learn of it and follow Vashti's example, Ahasuerus counters his concern by publicizing his humiliation to the world; in a move intended to show his power, he instead advertises to the entire empire that he cannot control his wife.[5] Finally, because of Vashti's demotion, he needs a new wife—one who will obey him better than Vashti did (1.19; 2.1–4). Esther is chosen and by appearing before Ahasuerus unbidden (cf. 4.11), she twice disobeys; each time, she is rewarded for it.[6] And ultimately, as an end result of *appearing before the king* unbidden, she wields far more control over the empire than Vashti ever threatened to by *not appearing before the king* when summoned; Ahasuerus rids himself of a wife who is a potential problem of authority only to find a replacement who—likely unbeknownst to him— had even more control.[7]

---

[3] Such overreaction is commonplace in the narrative and fits well in the category of satire, discussed below.

[4] Dillard and Longman, *An Introduction to the Old Testament*, 194.

[5] Bechtel, *Esther*, 25.

[6] Goldman, "Narrative and Ethical Ironies," 17.

[7] Moore, *Esther*, 14.

## 2. Rising and Falling

Much of the irony in Esther is centered on the theme of rising and falling that appears throughout the story.[8] The problem for the Jews began when Mordecai would not bow (i.e., *fall* down) before Haman (3.2ff) and escalated when he would not *rise* before Haman (5.9). In 3.7, when Haman cast the lot, the lot *fell* before Haman, thus determining what he thought would be the day of the Jewish genocide. After Mordecai would not *rise* before Haman (5.9), Haman erects a stake 50 cubits high to *raise* Mordecai up on (5.14). The turning point of the story is where Haman is forced to honor Mordecai (ch 6), which is also the ironic high point: Haman, intent upon Mordecai's death, becomes the unsuspecting instrument for Mordecai's exaltation.[9] Haman is told by Ahasuerus not to *fall short* in honoring him (6.10).[10] From this point forward, Mordecai rises as Haman falls. When Haman's wife, Zeresh, learns of Haman's humiliation before Mordecai, she says, "If Mordecai, before whom you have begun to *fall,* is of the Jewish people, you will not overcome him but *falling* you will *fall*" (6.13). At the second banquet Esther prepares, Haman *falls* on the couch (7.8), giving the appearance that he is assaulting Esther—and giving Ahasuerus a convenient excuse to dispose of Haman.[11] Haman's fall is paralleled

---

[8] See Forrest S. Weiland, "Literary Conventions in the Book of Esther," *Bibliotheca Sacra* 159 (October–December 2002): 433 for a detailed analysis of the theme of falling.

[9] Murphy, *Wisdom Literature,* 165.

[10] Often translated as something like "leave out nothing" (ESV).

[11] Bush, *Ruth, Esther,* 433 argues Ahasuerus could not have possibly thought Haman would have assaulted Esther, but "he chooses to so interpret Haman's action, thereby providing a charge with which to condemn him that relieves the king from raising publicly the true reason for the condemnation, the plot against the Jews."

by Mordecai's rise to the former's previous position.[12] Then, at what Weiland calls the most striking example of poetic justice, Haman is impaled—*raised up*—upon the stake he erected for Mordecai (7.10).[13] Finally, on the day (the lot *fell* to determine), Haman's sons and all the Jews' enemies *fell* before them (9.1, 5).

### 3. Haman's Plan

The death Haman wished on Mordecai and the Jews instead fell on him and his family: "The one who wanted to kill a Jew for not falling down before him was ultimately executed on a charge of falling down inappropriately before a Jew!"[14] To double the irony, he is condemned to death not for trying to kill the Jews, but for a crime he did not commit—attempted rape.[15] Ultimately, an irreversible edict calling for the extermination of the Jewish people was reversed so the Jews' enemies were exterminated.

In the next chapter, we will see the significance of irony as part of a larger series of ironic reversals that gives structure to the narrative and, in so doing, point toward the sovereignty of God. As Weiland says, "The turn of events and the timing of seemingly insignificant yet decisive occurrences seem so ironic that the reader must ponder the question, What has caused the reversal of all these things and why?"[16] The answer suggested

---

[12] Goldman, "Narrative and Ethical Ironies," 18.

[13] Weiland, "Historicity, Genre, and Narrative Design," 163. Weisman, *Political Satire in the Bible*, 154 adds that in his humiliation before Mordecai and falling before Esther, "Haman the Agagite, whom the king elevates and whose chair the king sets above all the princes, falls in a twofold and final manner, and his 'elevation' finds its ironic contrast in his being hanged from a tall tree in the sight of all."

[14] Duguid, *Esther and Ruth*, 90.

[15] Goldman, "Narrative and Ethical Ironies," 19.

[16] Weiland, "History, Genre, and Narrative Design in the Book of Esther," 163.

by the book's interbiblical, canonical context is that God is the cause of the reversal. Although Weisman says that even the casting of lots which fulfills so fundamental a role in the story is not supernatural but at most "non-natural,"[17] the canonical context suggests a supernatural force does stand behind the lot (Prov 16.33),[18] which is itself another irony since Haman likely believed the gods would determine the most fortuitous day for his plan to be executed by casting the lot.[19] Jobes sees a divine message in this providence, concluding that the ironic reversals show that, "despite their sin and their location away from Jerusalem, God's promise to Israel made at the beginning of their nation still stands. He will still destroy those who want to destroy his people, no matter where they are living."[20]

## B. Satire

The theme of irony also points to the satirical element in the narrative, since much of the ironic humor is at the expense of Ahasuerus and Haman. Likewise, the satire in the story is largely directed at Persian men of high rank, specifically Ahasuerus and Haman, though it also includes the king's advisors in Esther 1.

### 1. Ahasuerus

As previously noted, Ahasuerus claims great power and issues a decree that men should rule in their own houses, but he is

---

[17] Weisman, *Political Satire in the Bible*, 148.

[18] Baldwin, *Esther*, 23 argues Esther goes even further: "[E]ven when the dice had fallen the Lord was powerful to reverse its good omen into bad, in order to deliver his people."

[19] Weiland, "Literary Conventions," 432–433.

[20] Jobes, *Esther*, 42.

unable to master his own wife—neither Vashti nor Esther. He cannot even convince his wife to come to a party. As it turns out, "he is not only powerless; he is a bumbling buffoon who is surrounded by sycophants who convert a trivial dispute into a state emergency." [21]

In addition, Ahasuerus is perpetually unable to make any decisions on his own. When Vashti offends him in chapter 1, he calls together the wisest people available to help him determine what to do, bringing together "the legal experts and flower of Persia's aristocracy to formulate a response which any self-respecting male chauvinist could easily dream up for himself." [22] After Vashti's dethronement in chapter 2, Ahasuerus receives counsel regarding what to do next, and an "entire bureaucracy surrounds the choice of a royal bedmate." [23] In chapter 3, Haman convinces him to destroy an entire people without ever revealing who they are. Upon learning Mordecai has not been honored in chapter 6, Ahasuerus' first thought was to find out who was in the court who could tell him what to do to rectify the oversight. In chapter 7, Haman is hanged on his own gallows at the advice of a eunuch. Regardless of the disastrous previous grand vizier, Ahasuerus again happily turns over full decision making power to Esther and Mordecai in chapters 8 and 9. The only law the king writes without assistance is the utterly absurd decree that there was no law about drinking (1.8), a law to let others

---

[21] Firth, *The Message of Esther,* 37.

[22] Clines, *Ezra, Nehemiah, Esther,* 280. Missing this element of satire can have the unfortunate side-effect of leading an interpreter to say, as Karol Jackowski, "Holy Disobedience in Esther," *Theology Today* 45 no. 4 (1989): 408 does, "What follows could very well be viewed as the biblical foundations for the conspiracy to protect the male ego."

[23] Dillard and Longman, *An Introduction to the Old Testament,* 195.

do as they please.[24] In other words, his only decisions delegate power to others.[25] Throughout the book of Esther, Ahasuerus is a comical figure—a complete buffoon.[26]

About Ahasuerus' characterization, Fox points out that his psychology is easily read by the people *in* the story too: princes (ch 1), servants (ch 2), the grand vizier (ch 3), and his queen (chs 5–9) are all able to bend him to their wills, "for his moods and motives are obvious to all who must live by them, and he has no deeper resources to resist their blandishments."[27] Further, "[T]he all-powerful [Ahasuerus] in practice abdicates responsibility and surrenders effective power to those who know how to press the right buttons—namely, his love of 'honor,' his anxiety for his authority, and his desire to appear generous."[28]

Ahasuerus is the only character who appears in the story from beginning to end. He has the power of life and death, to dismiss and to choose, to promote and to execute. His seal authorizes edicts. Esther fears his potential wrath (4.11), and Haman is terrified before his actual anger (7.5).[29] Although he has this power, it is all superficial. As Weisman points out, "He does

---

[24] Laniak, "Esther," 195. Clines, *Ezra, Nehemiah, Esther,* 278 says, "In an autocracy, even the absence of a rule requires a decree!"

[25] Fox, *Character and Ideology,* 174.

[26] Bechtel, *Esther,* 26 cautions, "While it is true that his 'antics add an extra comic element,' it is also true that Ahasuerus is a dangerous man. Some of his danger derives specifically from his absurdity. ... In short, Ahasuerus may be a buffoon ... but he is a dangerous buffoon" (second ellipsis in original).

[27] Fox, *Character and Ideology,* 171.

[28] Ibid., 173.

[29] Much of the plot is driven by anger, including the principle narrative tension and its resolve: Haman's rage at Mordecai's refusal to bow and Ahasuerus' fury over Haman's "attack" of Esther. See Eliezar Segal, "Human Anger and Divine Intervention in Esther," *Prooftexts* 9 (1989): 248–249.

not take any initiative, he does not plan or act, and does not move the plot forward; he merely reacts to the initiative of others; and he himself is moved by his greed and by the effect others work upon him. He is the object, not the subject." [30]

## 2. Haman

If Ahasuerus is seen through a satirical lens, then Haman may be even worse. [31] In 3.2 a command has been issued that all bow to Haman. In addition to this being further evidence of the king's poor ruling (i.e., micromanagement), it may indicate a general lack of respect for Haman. [32] Haman may well be the only grand vizier in imperial history who needed a royal decree so the people would honor him! The quickness with which Harbona the eunuch suggests his own stake (7.9) also reflects poorly on both the king and Haman. It is one of many indications the king has little idea about what is going on in his city (cf. 3.15b; 6.10), and it also implies the palace staff does not like Haman any more than the general populace. [33] Like Ahasuerus, Haman is bested by his wife who first advises him to build gallows (5.14) and then speaks to his wounded ego, though not offering comfort as much as speaking of his imminent demise (6.13). Ultimately, Haman, "the gifted and successful one, the master

---

[30] Weisman, *Political Satire in the Bible*, 148–149. Weisman earlier suggested that the juxtaposition of 10.1 and 10.2—the taxation and "all the acts of his power and might"— may imply that the tribute is all that his power and might amounts to. He concludes, "Is it possible that in fact everything told in the story of his drunkenness and his lust for women, his capriciousness and his manipulation by courtiers, has produced this ironic acclaim?" (144).

[31] Webb, *Five Festal Garments*, 125 argues that "the most savage humour is at Haman's expense."

[32] Baldwin, *Esther*, 72.

[33] Ibid., 94.

planner, fails, and with him his plan. Not because he erred in elaborating any of its details, and not because he was suddenly punished from on high for his evil, but because he was caught in the meshes of a woman."[34]

Drawing on Robert Alter's study of opacity and transparency in the Saul/David story,[35] Fox points out that the reader is constantly informed of Haman's emotions, perceptions, nuances of his calculations, and even direct quotations of his thoughts with two scenes dedicated to showing just how his mind works (5.9–14; 6.1–11). He says, "The contrast between Haman and the other characters shows that the author is deliberately choosing to examine, and to throw a harsh light on, the squalid soul of the anti-Semite."[36] Later he describes the "disturbances of his psyche" as "a distended pride, a nervous insecurity, and an insatiable thirst for confirmation of his significance."[37] Fox says,

After the "high point" of his cleverness in chapter 3, everything Haman does is manifestly foolish, as he is buffeted about and driven by his passions and impulses. His anger makes him unable to wait for his revenge and leads him to push fate and try to kill Mordecai prematurely. The consequence is that he erects the instrument of his own death and rushes straight into humiliation. His fatuous assumption that he alone is worthy of the king's honors makes a public fool out of him. He, the vizier and high nobleman, has to conduct his enemy on horseback as his herald through the city square, all this exacerbated to the extreme by the fact that his conflict with Mordecai is well known among the palace officials who are watching the display. His folly finally unmasks itself

---

[34] Weisman, *Political Satire in the Bible*, 153.

[35] Alter, *The Art of Biblical Narrative*, 114–130.

[36] Fox, *Character and Ideology*, 179.

[37] Ibid., 182.

in his rash fall on Esther's couch, an act which is the immediate cause of his death. Haman is a buffoon, a clever fool.

By making Haman superficial and silly, the author hits him where his sort would most feel it: in his pride. We can imagine how a person such as the one created in this book would feel about the way he is depicted. Haman would not be bothered by being shown to be deeply evil, but he would be mortified to be revealed as an impulsive bungler.[38]

In this context, Fox recalls Charlie Chaplin's *The Great Dictator*, a satire of Hitler which denigrated his evil by showing him to be not only an evil and dangerous power, but also a "gesticulating, screeching, frenetic ninny ... exposing it for what it most deeply fears to be: weak within and ludicrous without."[39]

### 3. Drunkenness

The proliferation of alcohol is another place the Persians are satirized. In addition to the free-flowing alcohol at the banquet in Esther 1,[40] alcohol is involved in every subsequent decision: Ahasuerus decides to display Vashti when he was "merry with wine" (1.10); his decision to depose Vashti was (apparently) when they were all still in the same state of mind, his agreement to the genocide of an unnamed people was accompanied by drinking (3.15); and he made his offer of anything Esther requested, up to half of the kingdom, in the midst of drinking at both of her feasts (5.6; 7.2). While the use of alcohol in decision making

---

[38] Ibid., 183.

[39] Ibid., 183–184.

[40] Firth, *The Message of Esther*, 39 says, regarding the multiple banquets in Esther 1, "With the great feast finished one might think Ahasuerus would have had enough, but he seems to spend much of the book working on the theory that the best way to avoid a hangover is to stay drunk."

was a common feature of the Persian Court,[41] the Jewish reader would certainly see it as absurd, especially given the Wisdom literature's constant refrain on the dangers of alcohol.[42]

## 4. Excess

A final way the narrative satirizes the Persian world is through constant exaggeration and excess. This begins immediately with opulent descriptions of the court, feasts, and alcohol, as well as the king's unnecessarily large summons party for Vashti.[43] Upon her refusal, it is revealed in his—and his advisors'—overreaction to her rebuff: the multilingual, empire-wide publication of a law stating husbands should rule in their homes. The solution to Vashti's denouement—a dragnet, lining up all the virgins in the land for a multi-year sex contest[44]—is also clearly excessive. Haman's reaction to Mordecai's slight—genocide for a personal offense—is the point of excess on which the narrative tension is built.[45]

---

[41] Herodotus 1.133.

[42] Weisman, *Political Satire in the Bible*, 155 interestingly describes Haman's downfall as a result of being "drunk with success" that leads him to expose his weakness.

[43] Duguid, *Esther and Ruth*, 9 says, "With a characteristic touch of overkill, he sent no fewer than seven of the royal eunuchs who served him to summon his queen."

[44] Any description of Esther 2 as a "beauty contest" is either an attempt to edit the Bible story to a PG rating or simply fails to grasp the point of the narrative (e.g., Roland K. Harrison, *Introduction to the Old Testament* [Peabody: Prince Press, 1999], 1085: "[T]he king married the winner of what at the present day would be designated as a 'beauty contest'" or, worse, Jonathan Partlow, "Tough Decisions in the Silence of God: Esther 4.13–14," *Restoration Quarterly* 35 no. 4 [1993], 241–242: "They decided the most beautiful women in the kingdom would join a harem in the city, Susa, and have the biggest Mary Kay make-over party ever."). Unlike a beauty contest, entry was not optional and none of the "contestants" were allowed to go home, whether they won or lost (2.14).

[45] Some see Esther's request for a second day of killing as excessive (e.g., Paton, *Esther*, 287: "For this horrible request no justification can be found. A second massacre was in no sense an act of self-defence, since the power of the enemies of the Jews had already been

Even the language of the narrative contributes to the sense of excess. Berlin points to the exaggerated numbers (127 provinces, a 180-day party, a 12-month beauty preparation, Haman's offer of 10,000 talents of silver, a stake 50 cubits high, 75,000 enemies dead), long lists of unpronounceable names (the eunuchs, the advisors, the sons of Haman), flowery language ("What is your wish? It shall be granted to you. And what is your request? Even up to half the kingdom, it shall be fulfilled"), and bulky syntax ("If of Jewish stock is Mordecai, before whom you have begun to fall, you will not overcome him; you will surely fall before him"). She says,

> The rule for vocabulary, as for drinking, seems to be 'the more the better.' There are lot of 'alls' ('all the people who lived in the fortress Shushan,' 'every palace steward,' 'all the provinces,' 'all the women,' 'all the Jews,' 'all the king's servants') and the story never uses one word if it can use two. Dyadic expressions may consist of the same word used twice ('ish va-'ish, 'every man'; *medinah u-medinah*, 'every province'; *'am va-'am*, 'every people') or of synonyms joined together ('officials and courtiers,' 'the vast riches of his kingdom and the splendid glory of his majesty,' 'rest and deliverance,' 'light and gladness, happiness and honor'). One example of how this type of repetition may pile up is 8.17, whose literal translation is: 'In every province and province and in every city and city wherever the king's command and decree arrived, there was gladness and joy among the Jews, a feast and a holiday.'[46]

broken by the events of the thirteen of Adar" or more recently Judith Rosenheim, "Fate and Freedom in the Scroll of Esther," *Prooftexts* 12 [1992]: 132–133, who calls the charge of vindictiveness "irrefutable"). If, however, the original edict is taken at face value and Esther's request is understood in those terms (see, e.g., Robert Gordis, "Studies in the Esther Narrative," *Journal of Biblical Literature* 95 no. 1 [1976]: 49–53), it must be read as an act of self-defense, for that is all the original edict permitted; the second day is specifically a request for that edict to be in force for another day (9.13). Paton begs the question, presuming to know what the narrative does not explicitly reveal. It does, however, implicitly reveal by the continued fighting that the enemies had not, in fact, been broken.

[46] Berlin, *Esther*, xxvii.

Berlin goes on to argue "these stylistic features reinforce the sense that the story is a farce. They lend an air of comic burlesque to the description of the Persian court and to all that happens in it." [47]

The satirical element of the story has a twofold effect on the reader. On the superficial level, it engages in humorous mockery of the Gentile rulers. Beyond this, it may serve as a hint at divine providence: the most powerful men in the world have no real power or control at all; they are not the ones who are actually determining the outcome of the story. Firth says, "By showing the futility of such grandiose claims of human power, it opens up the question of where power really lies. ... If the greatest human power turns out to be a charade, then already there is a hint that real power lies elsewhere." [48]

## C. Foreshadowing

The key foreshadowing in Esther is found in a subtle historical context that clues the reader into where the story is heading. As already noted, Mordecai is introduced as a son of Kish, a Benjaminite (2.5) and Haman is introduced as an Agagite (3.1). [49] Haman and Mordecai are thus introduced in a historical context suggesting unfinished business that is rooted in the long-standing enmity between the Israelites and the Amalekites. As Moses already says in Exodus 17.16, "The

---

[47] Ibid., xxviii. Whether historicity should be determined by the farcical/satirical nature of the story is debatable. At the very least, there is certainly mockery of the Persian court going on in the narrative.

[48] Firth, *The Message of Esther*, 37.

[49] It is debated whether the Kish of Esther is the same Kish as King Saul's father and whether this Agagite is related to King Agag, but from a literary standpoint, the question is irrelevant. That the author chose to identify them thusly indicates to the reader at the outset that they will be enemies. See page 58n7, above.

Lord will have war with Amalek from generation to generation." Israel is then charged with "blot[ting] out the memory of Amalek from under heaven" (Deut 25.19; cf. Exod 17.14; 1 Sam 15.23). Throughout Israel's history, there is intermittent conflict with the Amalekites (Jdg 3.13; 5.14; 6.3, 33; 7.12; 1 Sam 27.8; 30.13–18) which comes to a head when Saul, *of the tribe of Benjamin and a descendant of Kish,* is instructed to annihilate the Amalekites *and their king Agag.* Saul, however, does not do this and loses his dynasty because of his failure to obey (1 Sam 15; 28.18), and so the two sides are still fighting during the time of Hezekiah (1 Chron 4.43).[50]

Haman's decree for the total destruction of the Jews is, in effect, his effort to do to Israel what Saul failed to do to the Amalekites.[51] But when the tables are turned at the end of the story, the Jews do not make the same mistake as Saul; they destroy their enemies and do not take any plunder. Deuteronomy 25.19 makes a connection between Israel having rest from her enemies and the destruction of Amalek. Another element of the literary artistry of the book of Esther—connecting it to the Old Testament story and to Israel's covenant God—is that when the Jews gain victory over their enemies, we find they received rest from their enemies (9.22).[52]

---

[50] Dillard and Longman, *An Introduction to the Old Testament,* 196–197.

[51] Ibid., 197.

[52] Ibid., 197.

# SIX

# The Centrality of Esther 6 as a Clue to God's Providence

Esther 6 serves as the central point in the Esther narrative. This is clear from the chiastic structure of the story as a whole, of which chapter 6 is the center point. Furthermore, Esther 6 is the pivot in a series of ironic reversals that run through the narrative. Esther and Mordecai's absence in this central chapter may also be a way the narrator detracts from their roles in the Jewish victory.

## A. Literary Structure

Authors often use literary structure to make the point of their story. Bar-Efrat says, "Structure has rhetorical and expressive value: it is one of the factors governing the effect of the work on the reader and in addition it serves to express or accentuate meaning."[1] Old Testament narratives are frequently structured as chiasms, and it seems Esther is no exception.[2]

---

[1] S. Bar-Efrat, "Some Observations on the Analysis of Structure in Biblical Narrative," *Vetus Testamentum* 30 (1980): 1972.

[2] The following chiastic structure of Esther is modified from David Dorsey *The Literary Structure of the Old Testament: A Commentary on Genesis–Malachi* (Grand Rapids: Baker Books, 1999), 163. The primary difference is that I have merged his units D and E, (and parallels) into a single unit D, D'. Dorsey concedes E' is "an admittedly weak match of unit E." Dorsey further breaks the book down into chiasms of chapters 1–6 and

**A**  King's proud feast (1.1–22)

　　**B**  Esther wins queenship (2.1–18)

　　　**C**  King's life is saved (2.19–23)

　　　　**D**  Haman's plot (3.1–4.17)

　　　　　**E**  Esther invites king and Haman to first banquet (5.1–14)

　　　　　　**F**  Haman's fortunes turn (6.1–14)

　　　　　**E'**  Esther invites king and Haman to second banquet (7.1–10)

　　　　**D'**  Haman's plot foiled (8.1–17)

　　　**C'**  Jews' lives are saved (9.1–10)

　　**B'**  Esther wins second day for Jews in Susa (9.11–19)

**A'**  Jews' feast of Purim established (9.20–10.3)

As is usually the case, the center point of the chiasm is the point of emphasis.[3] In Esther, the center point is chapter 6, where Haman's fortunes turn, starting a series of reversals which almost perfectly follow the same pattern of the chiasm, thus making it even more emphatic.[4]

If Esther were not framed in such a clear interbiblical context, one might suspect the heroes of the story are Esther and

---

chapters 6–10 with chapter 6 doing double duty, as the final unit of the former chiasm and the first unit of the latter. In the two sub-chiasms, the center points are Haman's Plot (3.1–15) and Haman's Plot Foiled (8.3–17). If there is merit to Dorsey's proposed structures, then the ironic reversals at the heart of these subsections may further point to divine providence at work. Breneman, *Ezra, Nehemiah, Esther,* 288 proposes a shorter chiasm with just three elements plus a center point, though the center remains at chapter 6. See also Levenson, *Esther,* 8 for another often-reproduced chiastic structure proposal with chapter 6 at the center.

[3] See Dorsey, *Literary Structure of the Old Testament,* 40–41.

[4] See page 96, below.

Mordecai: their rise to power within a foreign empire, Esther's planning and manipulation of Haman, Mordecai's staunch refusal to compromise his stance, the victory that resulted from their decree, and their institution of a new celebratory festival all point to their being the key figures and heroes of the narrative. Many interpreters, however, have seen the Esther narrative as a story of divine providence—God is the hero—as is the thesis of this book. As already noted, this view is suggested not only by God's conspicuous absence from the story[5] but also by the structure itself. Dorsey points out the significance of the turning point of the story (ch 6) not involving either Mordecai or Esther, which the reader might expect, but rather an ironic twist of fate in which the fortunes of wicked Haman begin to turn.[6] In fact, when Haman goes into Ahasuerus' presence, both Esther and Mordecai are completely helpless should the conversation turn in a different way. Esther has begun working out her plan,[7] but

---

[5] As I will argue in the next chapter, it is not merely the absence of God that points to his presence, but his absence at such key points in a book that engages with the rest of the Old Testament canon in such high frequency that points to his hidden workings.

[6] Dorsey, *Literary Structure of the Old Testament*, 164. Technically, Esther 6 does feature Mordecai, but, as Bush, *Ruth, Esther*, 417 points out, only as a foil to presage Haman's complete and utter downfall: "In the first scene [5.9–14, by Bush's outline] the narrator completes his characterization of Haman by depicting for us his monstrous obsession with his own position, power, and privilege through his gross overreaction to Mordecai's failure to give him the deference he regards as his due. In the second scene [6.1–11] Mordecai is the foil for the dramatic reversal in which Haman arrives to ask the king to hang Mordecai but instead must himself personally lavish upon Mordecai the public honor and recognition that he proposes for himself. In the third scene [6.12–14] Mordecai is again the foil for the complete reversal of the counsel of Haman's wife and friends, in which their confident advice in the first scene on how to effect Mordecai's demise becomes their somber prediction that Haman's public humiliation at Mordecai's hands presages his doom."

[7] See pages 118–122 below for an interpretation of Esther's plan that does not involve her being hesitant, afraid, or otherwise confused as she repeatedly pushes back making her request.

it will do little good to save her cousin if Haman is allowed to kill Mordecai the morning of the second banquet, however successful her plan might be in saving the rest of the Jews. Should Haman succeed, who knows whether Esther would have had the resolve to work out the rest of her plan? Clines says, "Here there is no room for human initiatives such as have been played out so adroitly in the previous scene. Now everything must be providential—or rather coincidental (which is the narrator's cipher for 'divinely arranged')."[8]

Haman, however, does not get to execute Mordecai; he is not even allowed to make his request. Instead, everything turns in the Jews' favor due to an unparalleled series of coincidences: the king happened to be sleepless that night; to cure his insomnia, he happened to ask to have the royal records read; the section that was read happened to be about Mordecai's good deed—when Mordecai had happened to overhear the assassination plot and Ahasuerus had happened to fail to reward him; Ahasuerus happened to decide to reward Mordecai rather than ignoring his previous oversight; Haman happened to be coming into the palace the next morning with a plan that happened to be the exact opposite of Ahasuerus' desire; Ahasuerus happened to ask for Haman's advice without naming the honoree; Haman happened to misread his intentions. And then everything falls apart for him.

At the turning point of the story—the key to everything unraveling for Haman and for building momentum in the Jews' favor—Esther and Mordecai are nowhere in sight. The point the structure of the book strongly implies is that even when he is unseen, God is in control. In the final analysis, none of these

---

[8] Clines, *Ezra, Nehemiah, Esther*, 307.

events *just happened;* they are not coincidences, but the working of God, the byproduct of his rule over history and nations. Although God is never named in the book, the structure reveals that it is about God from beginning to end.

## B. Reversals in Esther

The key literary element in the story, built out of the irony we previously saw, is *peripety*—a form of irony where an action or event intended or expected to produce a certain result instead produces its exact opposite.[9] In Esther, there are a series of such reversals throughout the story. While the reversals are typically not explicitly described as such, the narrator consciously draws attention to them by using identical or extremely similar phrasing in both the event and its opposite, most clearly emphasized at the high point of the resolution, Mordecai's counter-edict.[10]

The theme of reversal is, however, explicitly stated in 9.1 (emphasis added): "On the very day when the enemies of the Jews hoped to gain the mastery over them, *the reverse occurred:* the Jews gained mastery over those who hated them." Even though this is the only place it is so explicitly stated, "the reverse occurred" is a fitting description of what repeatedly happens throughout the story. The reversals roughly follow the same inverse parallel structure the book follows.[11]

---

[9] Bush, *Ruth, Esther,* 323.

[10] Ibid.

[11] Only the reversals in 8.15 and 8.17 are out of order. Contrary to the common approach to the reversals in Esther, Berg, *The Book of Esther,* 110 suggests that 4.13–14 is the turning point. Although it does occur between two fasts, two royal edicts, and two banquet pairs, it is not where the narrative takes its sharpest turn. Fox, *Character and Ideology,* 162 says, "In 4.13–14 (and, in fact, in 4.1), the danger has been addressed, but there is as yet no sign that it will be overcome. That sign, as Haman's associates recognize (6.13), comes with Haman's humiliation."

**3.1–2,** Haman's high rank

    **3.10,** Haman given signet ring

        **4.1,** Mordecai's mourning

            **4.3,** Fasting and weeping among the Jews

                **5.14,** Zeresh suggests gallows for Mordecai's hanging

                    **5.14,** Zeresh advises Haman concerning Mordecai

                        **6.6–9,** Haman seeks honor for himself

                        **6.11–12,** Haman forced to honor Mordecai

                        **6.13b–14,** Zeresh advises Haman concerning Mordecai

                        **7.9–10,** Harbona suggests Haman hung on his own gallows

                  **8.17a,** Feasting and celebration among the Jews

              **8.15a,** Mordecai's exaltation

            **8.2a,** Mordecai given signet ring

        **9.3–4; 10.3,** Mordecai's high rank

A closer look at the verses themselves reveals how specifically events are reversed. Identical phrases are set in italics.[12]

---

[12] From Bush, *Ruth, Esther,* 324.

**3.1–2,** King Ahasuerus promoted Haman son of Hammedatha, the Agagite. He advanced him in rank and gave him precedence over all his other nobles. And all the king's officials at court bowed down and did obeisance to Haman, for so the king had commanded.

**9.3–4; 10.3,** [Mordecai] had come to occupy a position of great power in the palace, while his fame was spreading through all the provinces. ...Mordecai was growing more and more powerful. ... Mordecai the Jew was second in rank only to King Ahasuerus himself and was preeminent among the Jews.

**3.10 ,** *Then the king took his signet ring* from his hand *and gave it to* Haman son of Hammedatha, the enemy of the Jews.

**8.2a,** *Then the king took off his signet ring* which he had taken from Haman *and gave it to* Mordecai.

**4.1,** Mordecai... tore his clothes, put on sackcloth and ashes, *went out into the* city, and raised a loud and bitter cry.

**8.15a,** Then Mordecai *went out from the* king clad in a royal robe of violet and white, wearing a large gold turban and a purple cloak of fine linen.

**4.3,** *And in every single province to which the command and edict of the king came, there was* great mourning *among the Jews, with* fasting, weeping, and lamentation, *while many* made their beds on sackcloth and ashes.

**8.17a,** *And in every single province* and every single city *to which the command and edict of the king came, there was* joy and gladness *among the Jews, with* feasting and celebration, *while many* of the peoples of the land professed to be Jews.

**5.14,** And his wife Zeresh and all his friends said to him, "Have a *gallows erected, fifty cubits high,* and in the morning speak to the king and *have Mordecai hanged upon it.* Then go with the king to the banquet full of joy."

**5.14,** And his wife Zeresh and all his friends said to him, "Have a gallows erected, fifty cubits high, and in the morning speak to the king and have Mordecai hanged upon it. Then go with the king to the banquet full of joy."

**6.6–9,** Haman thought, "Now, whom would *the king desire to honor* more than me?" So he said, "…let *royal robes* be brought which the king has worn and *a horse* which the king has ridden, with a royal diadem upon its head. *Let the robes and the horse* be given to a noble and *let him robe the man whom the king desires to honor and lead him through the city square and proclaim before him, 'This is what is done for the man the king desires to honor!'"*

**7.9–10,** Then Harbonah…said, "Look, the *gallows which Haman erected* for Mordecai, whose report benefitted the king, is standing at Haman's house, *fifty cubits high."* "Hang him on it!" said the king. *So they hanged Haman on the gallows* he had prepared for Mordecai.

**6.13b–14,** Then his advisers and Zeresh his wife said to him, "Since Mordecai, who has already begun to defeat you, belongs to the Jewish race, you will not get the better of him, but will most certainly fall before him." While they were still talking with Haman, the king's eunuchs arrived and brought him in haste to the banquet.

**6.11–12,** So Haman got *the robes and the horse.* He *robed Mordecai and led him through the city square* mounted on the horse. *And he proclaimed before him, "This is what is done for the man whom the king desires to honor!"* …And Haman hurried home mourning and in shame.

As Fox says, "While the aesthetic value of the antiphony is undeniable, the structure has a function that goes beyond aesthetics. It reflects and communicates the author's worldview."[13] While Fox ultimately argues the author's worldview is one that is uncertain about God, Bush disagrees. In line with what I argued in chapter 4 concerning the interbiblical context of Esther, Bush says the context of the book is "decidedly in favor of reading all of these elements as a statement about divine providence,"[14] pointing to the two fasts and Mordecai's "such a time as this" statement as the author's hints at the context being the "OT's world of faith." Second, he argues that *peripety* itself, "in which God acts to effect the reversal on behalf of his people," is a dominant Old Testament theme.[15] Jobes argues for providence from the center of the peripety as Dorsey argued it from the center of the structure:

> By making the pivot point of the peripety an insignificant event rather than the point of highest dramatic tension, the author is taking the focus away from human action. ... By [this], the characters of the story are not spotlighted as the cause of the reversal. This reinforces the message that no one in the story, not even the most powerful person in the empire, is in control of what is about to happen. An unseen power is controlling the reversal of destiny.[16]

Hence, this series of reversals, like the overall structure itself, suggests the providence of God working behind the scenes to ensure the safety of his people and the advancement of his cause. Additionally, it emphasizes chapter 6 as the center of the narrative.

---

[13] Fox, *Character and Ideology*, 163.

[14] Bush, *Ruth, Esther*, 325.

[15] Ibid.

[16] Jobes, *Esther*, 158.

# SEVEN

# Narrative Coincidences and God's Absence as Clues to God's Providence

## A. Coincidences

Nearly every expositor, whether writing a commentary or preaching a sermon, has noted the series of coincidences that run through the narrative. In Esther, events that initially appear to be merely incidental play a decisive role in the outcome, prompting the reader to ask why and how they happened, particularly whether it was by chance or if some "unseen and unmentioned power was superintending the affairs of the Jews."[1] Consider the following list:[2]

1. Vashti must refuse to appear before Ahasuerus

2. Ahasuerus must demote Vashti to make room for Esther

3. Esther must be brought into the king's contest

---

[1] Forrest S. Weiland, "Literary Clues to God's Providence," 36. Berg, *The Book of Esther*, 104 says, "These 'coincidences' fall within the realm of possibility but nevertheless strain the laws of credibility."

[2] Many authors compile such lists. See, e.g., Mark Lehman, "The Literary Study of Esther," 90; Forrest Weiland, "Literary Clues to God's Providence in the Book of Esther," 44; V. Hamilton, *Handbook on the Historical Books*, 540–542; J.W. McGarvey, "Divine Providence: Queen Esther," *McGarvey's Sermons: Delivered in Louisville, Kentucky June–September*, 1893 (Delight: Gospel Light Publishing, n.d.).

4. Hegai must notice Esther and advance her

5. Esther must be chosen by Ahasuerus[3]

6. Mordecai must be in the right place to hear about the assassination attempt

7. Ahasuerus must record Mordecai's good deed while failing to reward him

8. Esther must successfully hide her ethnicity

9. The lot must fall on a late day

10. Esther must be convinced by Mordecai to put her life on the line

11. Ahasuerus must accept Esther when she enters unsummoned

12. Esther must not immediately make her request, allowing for the events of chapter 6

13. Ahasuerus must have insomnia

14. Ahasuerus must decide to have the royal records read to him during his insomnia[4]

15. The section read must be the part that talks about Mordecai

16. Ahasuerus must decide to reward Mordecai

17. Haman must appear in the king's court at the right time

18. Ahasuerus must speak before allowing Haman to do so, being sufficiently oblique as to allow Haman's misinterpretation

19. Haman must misinterpret Ahasuerus to be speaking of him

---

[3] Weiland, "Literary Conventions," 433–434 points to the "favor" Esther continually experienced (2.9, 15, 17; 5.2; 8.4–5) as suggesting a providential power at work.

[4] The motive for this is never revealed—does he hope to get some work done while he cannot sleep or does he presume the history of his own reign is so boring it will provide a cure? Given the satirical aspect of the story, one cannot but suspect the latter may be the case.

20. Ahasuerus must return from the garden at the exact moment Haman is falling on Esther's couch

Given the canonical context of Esther and, in particular, the connections with the explicitly providential Joseph story (cf. Gen 45.5; 50.20), most interpreters understand this series of coincidences as suggesting the same providence. Weiland says, "At a minimum these dramatic developments and perfectly timed incidents allude to something more than chance. Taken together they suggest that a divine superintending and a providential weaving together of circumstances by an unseen hand have taken place."[5] Bush says of Esther 6, "A writer whose world view is that of the OT people of God (as so much else in the story has demonstrated is the case with the author of Esther) could only intend his reader to see the hand of divine providence in a series of events seemingly of such pure chance."[6] Even more strongly, Dillard and Longman say,

> What the writer of Esther has done is to give us a story in which the main actor is not so much as mentioned—the presence of God is implied and understood throughout the story, so that these mounting coincidences are but the by-product of his rule over history and the providential care for his people. It is an extraordinary piece of literary genius that this author wrote a book that is about the actions and rule of God from beginning to end, and yet that God is not named on a single page of the story.[7]

By contrast, Fox contends many stories pile up coincidences without investing any theological significance in them,[8] and the

---

[5] Weiland, "Literary Clues to God's Providence in the Book of Esther," 44.

[6] Bush, *Ruth, Esther,* 419.

[7] Dillard and Longman, *An Introduction to the Old Testament,* 196.

[8] Fox, *Character and Ideology,* 241.

author of Esther is uncertain about God's role in the events of the narrative.[9] Levenson, however, points out that Fox gives no examples of such stories from the literature of Second Temple Judaism and instead argues it to be "more reasonable that the author endorsed the old saw that 'a coincidence is a miracle in which God prefers to remain anonymous.'"[10]

## B. God's Conspicuous Absence at Key Moments

Those authors who read Esther in a religious light often find hints of God throughout the book, particularly in those passages where God is most conspicuously absent. These passages are, in my view, the least compelling reasons to see Esther as religious, but since they are nearly universally commented on, this section will briefly engage with a few such proposed indications of divine presence. Given the canonical context that has been established on the basis of the interbiblical connections already discussed, there may be more merit in considering them in this light than God's mere absence where he might be expected to be present.

### 1. "For such a time as this"

Mordecai's statement to Esther about her rise to her current position ("And who knows whether you have not come to the kingdom for such a time as this?" [4.14]) is likely the most famous verse in the narrative and frequently pointed to as evidence of Mordecai's religious leanings.[11] Baldwin represents this position

---

[9] Ibid., 247.

[10] Levenson, *Esther*, 19.

[11] Berlin, *Esther*, 44 rightly says, "God is most present and most absent in this chapter," though Firth, *The Message of Esther*, 70 contends "the book assumes God's activity, evident in God-shaped holes in the narrative." See page 72n55 above for discussion of the referent of "another place."

well: "Mordecai reveals that he believes in God, in God's guidance of individual lives, and in God's ordering of the world's political events, irrespective of whether those who seem to have the power acknowledge him or not."[12] Breneman also argues that this shows God's guidance in Esther's position as being queen, adding, "in the biblical perspective election is for service, not just for one's own benefit. Being liberator of her people was more important than being queen of Persia."[13]

### 2. Zeresh's statement

McClarty points out that Haman's wife, Zeresh, is the one who perceives prophetic significance in the events of the narrative. She discerns the Mordecai/Haman incident of Esther 6 as another link in the timeless rivalry between Jews and non-Jews—a son of Kish and a son of Agag—and analyzes the symbolism of Haman's recent humiliation.[14] Even Dunne, who warns against adding religion where it is not explicitly in Esther says Zeresh expresses the sort of covenantal theology we might expect from Mordecai or Esther.[15] Her statement—"If Mordecai, before

---

[12] Baldwin, *Esther,* 80. McConville, *Ezra, Nehemiah, and Esther,* 173 is even stronger: "Against the background of Israelite history Mordecai *can only* mean (a) that *God* has brought Esther to the present position in order to deliver his people, and (b) that if she will not do it then *God* will arrange it in some other way." Whitcomb, *Esther,* 78 also makes the case more strongly: "[I]t became suddenly clear to him in retrospect that God must have included all these remarkable events within His sovereign and unfailing plan." The problem with such strong statements of Mordecai's beliefs is they are juxtaposed against his own "Who knows?" See chapter 9 for more on Mordecai's "Who Knows?"

[13] Breneman, *Ezra, Nehemiah, Esther,* 337. Webb, *Five Festal Garments,* 123 argues this final question of Mordecai lifts Esther's responsibility to act "from a purely moral to a virtually religious level."

[14] Wilma McClarty, "Esther," *A Complete Literary Guide to the Bible* (Grand Rapids: Zondervan, 1993), 221.

[15] Dunne, *Esther and Her Elusive God,* 66. Dunne sees Zeresh functioning as a critique of the covenantal theology of the Jews. This only works if her silence about God

whom you have begun to fall, is of the Jewish people, you will not overcome him but will surely fall before him" (6.13)—certainly lends itself to being read in a providential way. Murphy calls it an anticipation of the eventual deliverance of the Jewish people, which he says is clearly its intention.[16] Beal adds that Zeresh's point is that anyone who opposes the survival of the Jews will fall.[17] Webb connects this statement with Mordecai's declaration of the Jews finding deliverance in another place. He argues that if Mordecai is certain the Jews will survive, Zeresh is equally certain their enemies will be destroyed: "There is no reference to any agent, human or divine; simply to an apparent law of history. ... It is the most absolute statement in the whole book that history as a whole has a pro-Jewish shape to it, and it is surely ironic that it comes, not from the Jews themselves, but from their enemies."[18]

This is another point where this book's emphasis on the interbiblical nature of Esther is illuminating. Fox points out in other canonical and apocryphal narratives, wisdom is placed in the mouth of Gentiles to show the truth about Israel and God is so certain and obvious that even neutral or hostile people recognize it (cf. Num 22–24; Dan 2.46–47; 3.28–33; 4.34; Judt

---

is allowed to be covenantal and Mordecai's silence be seen as proof of assimilation and secularity (or if Wiebe's view of Mordecai's statement—a rhetorical question expecting a negative answer—is correct).

[16] Murphy, *Wisdom Literature,* 165.

[17] Beal, "Esther," 86. He mitigates this some by the parenthetical addition, "whether by God's providence or by Jewish political savvy is another question." Forrest S. Weiland, "Plot Structure in the Book of Esther," *Bibliotheca Sacra* 159 (2002): 286 connects the "indestructability of the Jews," alluded to by Zeresh, with "all of the promises made to the Jews, particularly to the promise of bringing the Messiah into the world."

[18] Webb, *Five Festal Garments,* 123. This comparison only works if Wiebe's proposal of Mordecai's statement as rhetorical question is incorrect.

5.5–21; 2 Mac 9.12–27; 3 Mac 5.31; 6.25–28; 7.6–7).[19] In this light, Zeresh's statement should be seen as both generally religious and specifically pointing to providence.

### 3. Holy War

Chapters 8 and 9 have often been defended as Holy War and, in particular, a continuation of the ongoing war with the Amalekites. Among other reasons, the refusal to take plunder—particularly in the context of Saul's failure in that regard—leads some to make this connection.[20] Jobes represents this position: "[T]he author's emphatic statement three times over that the Jews did not lay a hand on the plunder suggests that this episode against Haman and those who 'hated' the Jews was understood as Holy War, not as an opportunity for looting and personal gain. The Jews of Persia succeeded where Saul failed."[21] Laniak makes the providential connection even stronger, saying, "For the narrator to imply that the Jews in Esther were following regulations for Holy War is to affirm that (1) God was fighting for them and that (2) this was a case of divine justice (not simply personal revenge)."[22]

---

[19] Fox, *Character and Ideology*, 79. Cf. Phillips, "Esther," 647. See Wells, "Esther," 68–69 for a further discussion of these passages.

[20] Esther's request to impale Haman's sons may also be a part of this motif, though it is less universally accepted. At the very least, it was a common practice in Ancient Near Eastern warfare and sometimes was part of the practice of Holy War carried out by Joshua (Josh 8.29; 10.26; cf. Duguid, *Esther and Ruth*, 115).

[21] Jobes, *Esther*, 198. Duguid, *Esther and Ruth*, 107 says, "Mordecai planned to finish what his ancient kinsman (see Est 2.5) had left incomplete. His edict was a continuation of that same ongoing struggle, of holy war." The refusal to take plunder might also indicate that Mordecai's inclusion of it in the original edict was only part of the full reversal of Haman's original decree, which also mentioned plundering. See Bush, *Ruth, Esther*, 442–443, 445, 453 for a fuller discussion of the parallel nature of the edicts. Bush ultimately argues against the connection based on taking/not taking plunder, but that it shows the Jews were motivated by self-preservation, not greed (477).

[22] Laniak, "Esther," 260.

## 4. Esther's Fast

The fast for which Esther calls should also be included here; it is often mentioned as evidence of religion in Esther because fasting is typically accompanied by prayer in the Old Testament.[23] It also seems quite sensible to connect the two because, after all, what good would it do Esther for all of her kinsmen merely to be hungry when she appears before Ahasuerus unbidden? On the other hand, Dunne marshals a strong case for this fast to be read in a secular context. He argues that fasting is often simply an expression of mourning: he cites 1 Samuel 31.13; 2 Samuel 1.12; 3.31, 35 and correlates it with Esther's presumption of her imminent death ("If I perish, I perish," 4.16).[24] Dunne concludes, "Fasting is not sufficient to make Esther 4 a religious context, we need the religious context first in order to interpret the fasting as religious."[25] While Dunne's conclusion may have merit, and the strength of his argument is what has led me to place this piece of evidence last in my list, I would counter that the argument of part two of this book—the interbiblical dialogue of chapter 4, in particular—may give us the very religious context Dunne seeks for interpreting the fast as religious.

---

[23] Baldwin, *Esther,* 80 says prayer is "always the accompaniment of fasting in the Old Testament." Cf. Keil, "Esther," 221, who quotes Berth: "Though 'God' and 'prayer' are not here mentioned, it is yet obviously assumed that it was before God that the Jews were to humble themselves, to seek his help, and to induce him to grant it. 1 Kings 21.27–29; Joel 1.14; Jonah 3.5f." Even Paton, *Esther,* 225 says, "Fasting can only be a religious act designed to propitiate God."

[24] Dunne, *Esther and Her Elusive God,* 49–50. Fasting's connection to mourning, however, does not necessarily disconnect it from religion. Often, mourning brings people to their most religious moments (cf. Ecc 7.1–4).

[25] Ibid., 50.

## C. Why Is God Excluded?

The question of why the narrator would choose to leave God out of the narrative remains. Although any proposed answer engages in some speculation, Weiland offers four helpful suggestions. First, the narrator may have chosen this method to emphasize the hidden nature of divine providence, which does not necessitate observable intervention and often appears invisible to human eyes. Second, the context of the recent captivity, where some Jews had chosen not to return and Mordecai initially prefers anonymity (2.10, 20), perhaps implying his own disassociation with God, may help clarify why God is hidden.[26] Third, omitting reference to God adds to the rhetorical irony the author uses. Finally, omitting reference to God emphasizes that God's care does not relieve people of the responsibility to act.[27]

In this light, especially given the context established over the last few chapters, it seems the argument that God's absence is proof of his presence may have merit after all—that what Paul says explicitly in Romans 8.28, the book of Esther "suggests through its consummate artistry."[28] As Clines says, "[T]here

---

[26] A different argument from the captivity context is suggested by Dave Bland, "God's Activity as Reflected in the Books of Ruth and Esther," *Restoration Quarterly* 24 no. 3 (1981): 141 who says that since no Jew would believe events happened by chance, the coincidences would make them realize Yahweh was behind their deliverance: "So the author's deliberate avoidance of religious language serves to catch the attention of a people who had been captive for so long, to remind them that Yahweh is still present in their lives."

[27] Weiland, "Literary Conventions," 429. On the fourth point, cf. Gregory R. Goswell, "Keeping God Out of the Book of Esther," *Evangelical Quarterly* 82 no. 2 (2010): 105–110 and David Beller, "A Theology of the Book of Esther," *Restoration Quarterly* 39 no. 1 (1997): 14.

[28] Francis C. Rossow, "Literary Artistry in the Book of Esther and Its Theological Significance," *Concordia Journal* 13 no. 3 (1987): 229.

is nothing *hidden* or *veiled* about the causality of the events in the Esther story: it is indeed *unexpressed,* but it is unmistakable, given the context within which the story is set."[29]

## D. Conclusion

In this section of the book, I have explored the interbiblical connections the author of Esther has integrated into the narrative, the literary features which may suggest the workings of God, the uncanny coincidences that run through the narrative, and a few other aspects of the story which are often taken as pointing to God's presence in the narrative. Foremost among the arguments is the interbiblical context within which the narrative is framed. This framing alone provides strong evidence that the author thinks his story should be read in those same terms. If this is the case, the narrator is not a "theological sophisticate promoting a 'religionless Judaism,' but an Old Believer whose ultimate act of faith is to take the protective providence of God for granted."[30] Once this reading is adopted, Mordecai need not be religious to convey religious ideas, and the literary clues and multiple coincidences within the narrative seem to clearly point to God.

---

[29] Clines, *The Esther Scroll,* 156.

[30] Ibid., 155–156.

# PART THREE

---

# Finding Practical Lessons in Esther

# EIGHT

# Esther: The Growth of Character Through Courage

In this book, I have, first, examined how Esther has been interpreted through the centuries, focusing particularly on the question of God's presence in the narrative. Second, I made an argument for it to be read as a religious document proclaiming God's providential work, primarily from the interbiblical framework in which it is written.[1] The final matter is how this argument should impact the modern reader.

In many ways, the twenty-first century Western Christian is in a similar situation to Esther and Mordecai: God seems largely silent—he does not appear visibly or speak audibly—and the believer is surrounded by a world whose values, by comparison, are upside down. What does the story of Esther reveal about how to live in such a world? In this final section, I will examine three basic ideas: first, I will explore the growth of Esther's character as a model of Christian growth that occurs within the framework of God's providential work; second, I will interact with Mordecai's "Who knows?" question, examining other similar biblical language as a model of Christian speech in the midst of God's silence; finally, I will consider Esther as a pattern for living in a pagan world.

---

[1] In an appendix, I will examine Esther 6 in detail, the chapter central to this theme.

Among the more fascinating analyses to come out of Esther research are the character studies done by Fox.[2] His study of Esther herself, in particular, is enlightening from a variety of perspectives, especially as it ultimately provides a very practical application for the modern Christian. The key feature in the character of Esther is her growth: by the end of the story, she is not the person she was at the beginning. Fox traces her character development through three distinct phases, which this chapter will follow before drawing ministerial applications.

## A. Passivity

At the beginning of the story, Esther is a completely passive character. This is shown in a variety of ways. First, the introduction of Esther into the narrative is noteworthy:

> Now there was a Jew in Susa the citadel whose name was Mordecai, the son of Jair, son of Shimei, son of Kish, a Benjaminite, who had been carried away from Jerusalem among the captives carried away with Jeconiah king of Judah, whom Nebuchadnezzar king of Babylon had carried away. He was bringing up Hadassah, that is Esther, the daughter of his uncle, for she had neither father nor mother. The young woman had a beautiful figure and was lovely to look at, and when her father and her mother died, Mordecai took her as his own daughter. (Est 2.5–7)

Rather than actually being introduced herself, she is introduced incidentally during the introduction of Mordecai, and as the object of his action—he "was bringing" her up and "took her as his own daughter."[3] In this non-introduction, she is de-

---

[2] Fox, *Character and Ideology*, 164–234.

[3] Ibid., 197. Mordecai is clearly the "main character" in the book. In addition to receiving the only real introduction, Mordecai also is the last figure praised. Weisman, *Po-*

fined mostly by how she looks[4] and by the death of her parents. Throughout Esther 2, she is completely compliant with everyone, from Mordecai whom she obeys (2.10, 20) to Hegai who advises her on what to take with her to the palace (2.15) to, presumably, Ahasuerus himself, whose sexual whims she satisfied above all the other women in the land (2.13–14, 16–17).

The compliant nature of Esther is further emphasized by the fact that nearly every time she appears in chapter 2, Esther is the passive object of someone else's action. She is taken into the harem (2.8); Hegai advances her (2.9); things are "happening to her" (2.10); she is taken to the king (2.15); she is made queen (2.19). The one exception to this passivity is her "winning favor" (2.9, 15), something many commentators point to as an unusually active expression,[5] given that other biblical characters usually "find favor," which seems to be a more passive concept.[6] While this expression may indicate "she is somehow actively attracting and engaging those around her in

---

*litical Satire in the Bible,* 154 also points out he is central in the development of the events related to the "lots" (Purim) and that the festival itself is later known as "Mordecai's Day" (2 Mac 15.31). See also B.D. Lerner, "No Happy Ending for Esther," *Jewish Biblical Quarterly* 29 no. 1 (2001): 11 who argues that, at the end, while "Ahasuerus is busy exploiting his subjects, and Mordecai basks in the glory of his political success ... Esther's happiness and even her personal piety are expendable. She remains trapped in the palace and bedroom of a drunken Persian King. ... There is no happy ending for Esther."

[4] Frederic W. Bush, "The Book of Esther: Opus non gratum in the Christian Canon," *Bulletin for Biblical Research* 8 (1998): 49 says, "She begins as a non-entity, valued in that courtly world only for her good looks and her body."

[5] E.g., Fox, *Character and Ideology,* 31: "This idiom (found only in Esther) holds a suggestion of activeness in 'gaining' rather than, as the usual idiom has it, 'finding' (*maṣaʾ*) kindness. Gaining kindness is something she is doing, rather than something being done *to* her."

[6] The LXX translates 2.9 as εὗρεν χάριν ("found favor") as well. Since the passive "finding favor" is sometimes framed theologically (cf. Dan 1.9), this may be another subtle religious addition to the LXX.

ways that bring her benefit,"[7] it may be an ironic way of saying her passivity is what "actively" garnered this approval. After all, Vashti stood up for herself, shaking the very foundations of the empire (or so the men's reaction would suggest), and was deposed. The search was for a new queen who would be "better than she" (1.19). In this context, "better" may be best understood as more willing to toe the royal line. Thus, Esther wins favor not by actively winning it, but by "fitting into the agenda that the empire set for her"[8]—in this case, by being completely compliant in every way.

Another way her passivity is emphasized is in her induction to the harem. Fox says,

> [T]he way the induction is described suggests docility of the deepest sort. If she had been dragged off weeping, she would at least have been expressing indignation at having her sexuality—indeed, her whole life—expropriated by the royal authority. Or if she had gone off pleased at her prospects for personal promotion, she would at least have been lending her will to the bargain. But unlike the men at the banquet (1.8b), Esther is not consulted; her will is of no interest. The author does not even hint at how Esther felt about what was happening to her, because her feelings are irrelevant. But this ostensive indifference to Esther's soul is not because the author is indifferent to her as an individual; the contrary will be proved in the course of the book as in 4.10–16, where her hesitation, fear, and resolution are crucial to the progress of the story. Rather, the author seeks to convey the insignificance of her will and mind *at this stage*. Esther is putty.[9]

---

[7] Laniak, "Esther," 207.

[8] Duguid, *Esther and Ruth*, 23.

[9] Fox, *Character and Ideology*, 197.

The situation begins to change, however, in Esther 4, which marks her transition from passivity to activity. Here, Mordecai has learned about Haman's edict for the extermination of the Jews and shows up at the king's gate in sackcloth and ashes. Esther sends him clothes, presumably so he could enter the king's gate,[10] and maybe even so they could meet to discuss whatever was upsetting him. When he refuses the clothing she sends, she communicates with him through Hathach, one of the king's eunuchs. In this scene, she suddenly begins to take initiative: she sends garments (4.4); she calls for and commands Hathach (4.5); she inquires of Mordecai (4.5); she again commands Hathach (4.10). While these active behaviors may not seem like much—especially for a queen—it is a significant advancement for Esther, who had always and only been passive.

In addition, Esther shows significant advancement in this chapter by displaying her feelings. Before, she unquestioningly—without any reported emotion—did whatever she was told in every instance. Now, as Fox says, "For the first time, we start to identify with her as a person and to see events through her eyes."[11] We first get a glimpse into her psyche when we find her concerned for her own safety at the prospect of going to the king unbidden (4.11).[12] Mordecai's response also shows a significant step forward, as "he argues with her, gives her evidence, and seeks to persuade her. He is beginning to treat her not merely as a former ward but as a partner, an adult and equal who must be persuaded

---

[10] Reid, *Esther,* 100. As opposed to Duguid, *Esther and Ruth,* 47 who sees her as wanting him to stop "making an exhibition of himself."

[11] Fox, *Character and Ideology,* 198.

[12] Ibid., 199 points out that she does not yet fully identify with her people, which is "hardly surprising, for she has lived apart from them for over four years, during which time she has carefully concealed her identity."

rather than commanded."[13] This change is something most parents can appreciate: at an early age, children obey simply because they are told to do so, "because I said so" is sufficient, and explanations often mean little to toddlers. As children grow, however, reasons for commands are given along with the command. Once they leave home, commands are difficult to enforce and often not appreciated; parents, instead, are left to reasoning and persuasion as their children are fully independent of their will. Esther is at this stage, and Mordecai realizes she must think through the matter and decide on her own what course to take.

## B. Activity

After a chapter of transition, the final turning point is "abrupt and surprising. She resolves to do her duty, and a change immediately comes upon her."[14] Here, she commands Mordecai, and he obeys her (4.15–17), a clear mark of changed status from previous interactions. Beyond that, she organizes a community wide fast, "assuming the role of a religious and national leader, and doing so prior to Mordecai's own assumption of that role."[15]

In addition to this immediate leadership, she begins to devise and work out a plan. Contrary to popular retellings of the story where Esther is nervous and uncertain about what to do,[16] the

---

[13] Ibid.

[14] Ibid.

[15] Ibid.

[16] E.g., McGarvey, "Divine Providence," 238 who says of the first banquet request, "I suppose she was afraid to [ask for Ahasuerus to save her people], for fear he would say no"; Whitcomb, *Esther*, 84, who sees her as "perhaps sensing that she did not yet have sufficient influence with the king" and suddenly deciding to postpone her request; and J. Vernon McGee, *Ezra, Nehemiah, and Esther*, Thru The Bible Commentary Series (Nashville: Thomas Nelson, 1991), 224 who says of the second banquet, "Esther still does not have the courage to express her request to the king."

two banquets she holds for Ahasuerus and Haman are part of a carefully constructed plan. It is clear at the outset that Esther is "biding her time rather than losing her nerve"[17] because the first banquet is already prepared (5.4). It is also clear, as will be shown, from her request at the first banquet that it is not, as Paton suggests, purely literary, allowing time for Haman's humiliation before the final blow falls.[18]

Esther's plan has at least two levels. First, there is the inclusion of Haman. She could not make such an accusation against Haman without him present. Any gap of time between the accusation and the resulting confrontation with Haman would have allowed time for Ahasuerus' anger to cool, and she could not have pressed her advantage.[19] Also, she could not guarantee her presence at the later confrontation, and who knows how Haman could have excused himself from danger when it was "just the boys" sitting around drinking wine. In addition, her inclusion of Haman at the banquets may have had the function of arousing Ahasuerus' jealousy with the intent of turning the king against him. McConville points out that although the first dinner is "for the king" (5.4), the second is "for the king and Haman" (5.8). He says, "There is just a hint here that Esther's purpose is to sow resentment in the king's mind, and have him think that this Haman was staking too big a claim in both the kingdom and in his wife's esteem."[20]

Second, Esther shows she is working out a plan by the way she conducts the banquets. As noted, the first banquet was al-

---

[17] Reid, *Esther*, 107.

[18] Paton, *Esther*, 234.

[19] Bechtel, *Esther*, 53.

[20] McConville, *Ezra, Nehemiah, and Esther*, 177.

ready prepared when she made her first request to Ahasuerus, which shows she is not merely afraid or stalling; rather, the first banquet is part of the plan. While the second banquet might seem merely like a delay tactic, her purpose becomes clear upon a close examination of what she says: "If I have found favor in the sight of the king, and if it please the king to grant my wish and fulfill my request, let the king and Haman come to the feast that I will prepare for them, and tomorrow I will do as the king has said" (5.8). Notice what she says: "If you will grant my wish, come to the feast." As Laniak points out, "Through a skillful use of language, the queen persuades the king to agree to her ultimate request *by accepting her invitation to the second banquet.*" [21]

At this point, Esther holds all the cards. She is in control of the timing as she has Haman rushed to both the first banquet and the second (5.5; 6.14).[22] She is in control of the events, as is evident when the king and Haman, literally, do "according to the word of Esther" (5.5). Before even asking, she has what is essentially a promise to grant her request—and she has been able to frame what she wants as "what the king has said" (5.8).[23]

Finally, the second banquet comes. At this one, she makes her accusation, leaving Haman "terrified before the king *and queen*" (7.6). Her success has come from a carefully calculated and enacted plan. Fox describes her strategy and rhetorical skill very well:

> [T]he best explanation for Esther's delaying her request until the second banquet is that she is unfolding a premeditated strategy; and once we grant this, we are justified in scrutinizing her words

---

[21] Laniak, "Esther," 233.

[22] Laniak says the haste is a subtle hint that Esther is taking charge (Ibid.).

[23] Clines, *Ezra, Nehemiah, Esther,* 305.

for further signs of this plan. Such a scrutiny shows her building up to the accusation with great care: piquing the king's suspense, eliciting a near-promise to fulfill her wish, withholding information that could put the king on the defensive (by making him face his own culpability), delaying other information (the identity of the offender) until she has given full momentum to the king's anger, softening her speech with deferential courtesies and demurrals that play to his ego, cracking out her accusation like a whip, then allowing matters to take their course once she has set Haman careening toward destruction. ... At the conclusion of Esther's plea, Haman is exposed and shaking in terror—not only before the obvious power holder, the king, but also before the queen (7.6). She is now a force to be reckoned with in her own right.[24]

Sasson also offers a helpful summary of the unfolding plan and its result:

By itself, Esther's accusation of personal malice might only have led the king to investigate the matter, as he did earlier in similar circumstances (2.23). The king himself might not have decided instantly to impale Haman if he had not very recently remembered Mordecai's loyalty. With Harbona's revelation, right after Haman's clumsy lurch at the queen, that Haman has prepared a (seventy-five-foot!) stake for Mordecai, the evidence for a conspiracy fully crystallizes in the king's mind. Moreover, the scene realizes its comic potential through the contrast between two separate points of view: that of the king, who grows increasingly suspicious, and that of Haman, who, even to the last, never knows why the king, let alone Esther, turns against him.[25]

At this point, Esther is a far cry from the passive wallflower the reader met in chapter two. No longer a pawn to be moved

---

[24] Fox, *Character and Ideology*, 201–202.

[25] Sasson, "Esther," 340.

around at someone else's whim, she is, indeed, the queen, able to move wherever she likes and to bring fear to anyone who would stand against her.

## C. Authority

The final stage of Esther's development, which is less significant to the purpose of this book, is one of authority. Ahasuerus empowers her by giving her control of Haman's property (8.1). Esther then reveals her relationship with Mordecai, upon which he is promoted to grand vizier, and she puts him over the estate of Haman. That she becomes the source of wealth and power for Mordecai further restructures their relationship and raises her status.[26]

Her authority is also seen in the massacre of the Jews' enemies. After a day of successful fighting, Esther asks that they be given another day to defend themselves and that the bodies of Haman's sons be impaled (9.13). In this scene, Ahasuerus is quick to give Esther her way, and she readily accepts his offer (9.12).

Finally, after the Jews' victory, the feast of Purim is established, and Esther's letter validates this new festival (9.29–32).[27] The only Jewish festival not included in the Law of Moses is inaugurated by Esther herself.

## D. Application

Not all characters in the Bible are heroes and great pillars of faith. In fact, most have foibles that become evident at some

---

[26] Fox, *Character and Ideology*, 202. I say "further" here on the basis of his reasoning with her instead of commanding her and his obeying her commands in Esther 4.

[27] See Ibid., 204 for a discussion of the textual problems in this passage. Fox concludes that either way it is read indicates Esther is the final authority in the feast of Purim.

point. Esther's morality has been questioned from a variety of angles, and while it may be difficult to know exactly where she and Mordecai stood before God, they are depicted as ordinary people trying to get by in a pagan world, people who are sometimes willing to allow themselves to blend in with the crowd. This fact is precisely why their story is so relevant to the modern reader, who is also an ordinary person trying to get by in a pagan world and, most likely, sometimes willing to allow himself or herself to blend in with the worldly crowd.

The lesson of Esther's character development is that ordinary people can do remarkable things. She played an important role in helping to deliver her people, but did not do so by her own miraculous working or a deep inner faith that was always at the forefront of her life and visible to everyone around her. Instead, she rose to the moment by becoming a better person. Fox says, "Esther becomes a sort of judge (of the type we see in the book of Judges) without benefit of the Spirit of the Lord. She is a leader whose charisma comes not in a sudden divine imposition of spirit but as the result of a difficult process of inner development and self-realization."[28] In short, she adapted to her circumstances using every resource at her disposal to become what her family and her nation needed her to be at that moment. She became something she initially was not, likely leaving her "comfort zone" to do difficult, and potentially life-threatening, work.

Although this lesson of adaptation and growth may be a simple one to grasp conceptually, it is often much more difficult to implement. Christians, however, must learn and practice this lesson. In all of our lives, we face the danger of settling into

---

[28] Fox, *Character and Ideology*, 205.

ruts of comfort, when the Christian life is supposed to be one of continual self-denial (cf. Luke 9.23; Rom 12.1–2; Phil 2.3–4; etc.) for the service of others. Thus, the Christian must find out what his family and his church needs him or her to be and grow into that person, regardless of comfort zones or circumstances— mostly by growing, and helping the church grow, into the very image of Christ himself (Eph 4.12–16).

---

# NINE

# "Who Knows?"
## A Biblical Response to God's Sovereignty

Christians have a tendency to view God in two extremes: they are either essentially deists who do not see God as interacting with his creation at all, or they are certain God has a hand in every detail of life, and his workings can be seen in even the smallest minutiae. As is often the case in matters with extreme positions, the truth may be somewhere in the middle. Contrary to the deist, the Bible does affirm God is an active participant in the world today. On the other hand, it leaves some uncertainty about his dealings with the world. The following examples of biblical speech regarding God's activity in the world give a helpful guide to how Christians today can express faith in God while remaining humble to his sovereignty.

### A. Mordecai

Mordecai's famous question—*"Who knows* whether you have not come to the kingdom for such a time as this?"* (4.14b)—may seem to be a difficult passage to get to the heart of. First, one must determine whether Esther is to be read religiously or not. This book has already argued it should be, and thus either Mordecai or the narrator intends this to be a providential statement.

Second, one must understand whether Mordecai is being positive or negative; in particular, as discussed,[1] whether 4.14a is a statement of faith or a rhetorical question presuming a negative answer as motivation for Esther to act. Surprisingly, even those who see 4.14a in a negative light still see 4.14b as a declaration of God's providential working in the life of Esther.[2] Yet, rather than presuming upon God, Mordecai only suggests.[3] This characteristic of the faithful not presuming upon God is a theme that runs consistently through the Bible. On several other occasions, biblical characters will ask this identical question: "who knows?"

## B. David

After David's sin with Bathsheba, God told him through the prophet Nathan that the child conceived in that sin would die. The child was born and fell ill, so David began to fast and pray and did so for a week until the child died, at which point David worshipped, went home, and ate (2 Sam 12.14–20). The servants, who were first afraid to tell David of the child's death, were completely shocked by his behavior. His response is, "While the child was still alive, I fasted and wept, for I said, '*Who knows* whether the LORD will be gracious to me, that the child may

---

[1] See pages 72–73, notes 55–57, above.

[2] E.g., Bush, *Ruth, Esther,* 400 says, "[H]e makes the suggestion ... that there is providential purpose in her position."

[3] This is in stark contrast to Whitcomb, *Esther,* 78 who, on the basis of Mordecai's "who knows," says that "it became suddenly clear to him in retrospect that God must have included all of these remarkable events within his sovereign and unfailing plan." As Tom Hamilton, "The Book of Joel," *Minor Prophets I: Hosea–Micah,* Truth Commentaries (Bowling Green: Guardian of Truth Foundation, 2007), 412 says regarding a similar statement in Joel 2, it is inexplicable that some "take this to be an assertion of certainty ... when it is patently just the opposite."

live?' But now he is dead. Why should I fast? Can I bring him back again? I shall go to him, but he will not return to me" (2 Sam 12.22–23). David does not accept Nathan's message in a fatalistic manner, as if God were impervious to human pleas,[4] but at the same time does not presume his special covenant relationship with God or status as Israel's king or hymn-master or "the man after God's own heart" earned him any favors. He simply expresses hope, admitting he does not know exactly what God will do.

## C. Joel

Joel follows the pattern of most of the pre-exilic prophets: indictments for sin to show the people have broken the covenant (particularly idolatry, religious ritualism, and social injustice); declarations of judgment; and brief glimpses of a hope of restoration.[5] One of these glimpses of hope is in a call to repentance:

> "Yet even now," declares the LORD,
>> "return to me with all your heart,
> with fasting, with weeping, and with mourning;
>> and rend your hearts and not your garments."
> Return to the LORD your God,
>> for he is gracious and merciful,
> slow to anger, and abounding in steadfast love;
>> and he relents over disaster.
> *Who knows* whether he will not turn and relent,
>> and leave a blessing behind him,

---

[4] J.G. Baldwin, *1 and 2 Samuel: An Introduction and Commentary*, Tyndale Old Testament Commentaries (Downers Grove: IVP Academic, 1988), 257.

[5] See J. Daniel Hays, *The Message of the Prophets: A Survey of the Prophetic and Apocalyptic Books of the Old Testament* (Grand Rapids: Zondervan, 2010), 62–69 for a summary of this basic prophetic pattern among the preexilic prophets.

a grain offering and a drink offering
  for the LORD your God? (Joel 2.12–14).

Here again is the "who knows" question. This statement, according to Hubbard, is "a humble way of holding out hope. This is no time for presumption, but it is a time for anticipation, held in check by awe of God's sovereignty."[6] Even in the midst of countless appeals for repentance and the constant prophetic assurance that God would take them back, Joel does not presume upon God but only speaks to the possibility, indicating the freedom and sovereignty of God, knowing that while people may hope for his compassion, they cannot command it.[7]

### D. The King of Nineveh

Jonah is unique to the prophetic books in that it is mostly narrative. The prophetic message itself is very brief—just one sentence: "Yet forty days, and Nineveh shall be overthrown!" (Jon 3.4). It is also unique in that, unlike every other prophetic book, the audience listened and repented![8] To ensure the repentance of his people, the king issued a decree: "By the decree of the king and his nobles: Let neither man nor beast, herd nor flock, taste anything. Let them not feed or drink water, but let man and beast be covered with sackcloth, and let them call out mightily to God. Let everyone turn from his evil way and from the violence that

---

[6] David Allan Hubbard, *Joel and Amos: An Introduction and Commentary,* Tyndale Old Testament Commentaries (Downers Grove: Intervarsity Press, 1989), 58.

[7] Douglas Stuart, *Hosea–Jonah,* Word Biblical Commentaries (Nashville: Thomas Nelson, 1987), 252.

[8] The larger point of Jonah's inclusion in the Hebrew canon may be to indicate just how hopelessly lost Israel was. In Nineveh, everyone repented—from king down to the cattle! (4.6–8)—whereas in Israel, God's prophets were, at best, ignored, but often mocked and killed.

is in his hands. *Who knows?* God may turn and relent and turn from his fierce anger, so that we may not perish" (Jon 3.7–9).

Just like Joel, the king of Nineveh does not presume upon God's forgiveness, but seeks after him hopefully. Accordingly, Alexander says, "[T]he king and his nobles acknowledge the absolute freedom of God to do as he pleases. ... God is under no obligation to pardon. There remains, however, the hope that he may look upon them with mercy and turn away his fierce anger. A complete turnabout by the Ninevites (v 8) may possibly encourage God to do likewise." [9]

### E. "Perhaps"

In addition to these "who knows" statements, the Bible is replete with the faithful saying what God will "perhaps" or "may" do. While this is not an exhaustive list, perhaps it will be sufficient to illustrate the theme.

First, in the context of forgiveness, parallel to Joel 2 and Jonah 3:

The next day Moses said to the people, "You have sinned a great sin. And now I will go up to the LORD; *perhaps* I can make atonement for your sin." (Exod 32.30)

Hate evil, and love good,
    and establish justice in the gate;
*it may be* that the LORD, the God of hosts,
    will be gracious to the remnant of Joseph. (Amos 5.15)

Seek the LORD, all you humble of the land,
    who do his just commands;

---

[9] T. Desmond Alexander, "Jonah: An Introduction and Commentary," *Obadiah, Jonah, Micah,* Tyndale Old Testament Commentaries (Downers Grove: Intervarsity Press, 1988), 124.

> seek righteousness; seek humility;
> > *perhaps* you may be hidden
> > on the day of the anger of the LORD. (Zeph 2.3)

In addition to forgiveness, it also occurs in the context of God's more general dealings with mankind, parallel to 2 Samuel 12 and Esther 4:

> "So now give me this hill country of which the LORD spoke on that day, for you heard on that day how the Anakim were there, with great fortified cities. *It may be* that the LORD will be with me, and I shall drive them out just as the LORD said." (Josh 14.12)

> Jonathan said to the young man who carried his armor, "Come, let us go over to the garrison of these uncircumcised. *It may be* that the LORD will work for us, for nothing can hinder the LORD from saving by many or by few." (1 Sam 14.6)

> For this *perhaps* is why he was parted from you for a while, that you might have him back forever, no longer as a bondservant but more than a bondservant, as a beloved brother—especially to me, but how much more to you, both in the flesh and in the Lord. (Phlm 15–16)

Each of these contexts reflects the same perspective of faith in God's dealings with humankind while conceding to God's sovereignty: whether a military leader like Caleb or Jonathan, a prophet like Moses, Amos, or Zephaniah, or even the apostle Paul,[10] people of faith acknowledge God's working, but do not

---

[10] Although Paul does not mention God as the subject of the verb, he uses the passive voice, which, in addition to being a euphemism for Onesimus' illegal flight, is used in the New Testament to denote God's agency. See David E. Garland, *Colossians and Philemon,* The NIV Application Commentary (Grand Rapids: Zondervan, 1998), 333; Douglas J. Moo, *The Letters to the Colossians and to Philemon,* The Pillar New Testament Commentary (Grand Rapids: Eerdmans, 2008 ), 419; etc.

presume to know all of the details of why things happen the way they do. In short, "maybe," "perhaps," and "who knows" do not indicate a lack of faith but a commitment to humility in regard to God's sovereign working.

## F. Joseph's Certainty

There is, however, at least one instance of a man of faith clearly claiming to know what God was doing. Twice, Joseph tells his brothers God was behind his long sojourn in Egypt.[11] Joseph's life is an excellent illustration of the principle that there are two aspects to any event, human mishandling and the perfect will of God, and to draw the reader's attention on "the latter as alone of being any consequence."[12] At this point in his life, Joseph has come to understand that God's purposes are fulfilled through and in spite of the choices of mankind, whether good or evil,[13] and that God "directs the maze of human guilt to achieve his good and set purposes."[14]

What is not revealed, however, is *when* Joseph came to realize this. It is reasonable to presume he likely prayed for many nights as he lay awake in Potiphar's house that his wealthy, powerful father would come to rescue him—not knowing his father believed him to be dead—before finally giving up on that

---

[11] When Joseph first reveals himself to his brothers, he says, "[Y]ou sold me here, [but] God sent me before you to preserve life" (Gen 45.5; cf. vv 7–8). After Jacob's death, when the brothers are again afraid of reprisal, Joseph says, "[Y]ou meant evil against me, but God meant it for good" (Gen 50.20).

[12] Derek Kidner, *Genesis: An Introduction and Commentary,* Tyndale Old Testament Commentaries (Downers Grove: Inter-Varsity Press, 1967), 207.

[13] Gordon J. Wenham, *Genesis 16–30,* Word Biblical Commentary (Dallas: Word, 1994), 432.

[14] Bruce K. Waltke, *Genesis: A Commentary* (Grand Rapids: Zondervan, 2001), 563.

hope.[15] Hamilton is correct that nothing in the narrative prepares us for Joseph's eloquent theologizing and that he likely came to understand God's working in his life slowly over the twenty years he was in Egypt.[16]

## G. Application

As mentioned above, the discussion of God's activity in the world tends toward extremes: either one suggests a nearly deistic God who does nothing or God is a micro-manager who opens up parking places and turns traffic lights green. The witness of Scripture, however, affirms neither. This is certainly not to deny God's ability or willingness to involve himself in human life at this level; rather it is to affirm that humans cannot definitively know what God is doing. As with Joseph, Scripture allows for human evil, while also showing God is in control of the outcome. It also acknowledges some events in life are the working of Satan (e.g., Job 1; John 13.27), while simultaneously showing the sovereignty of God in the process (e.g., Job 2.3; Acts 2.23). It further teaches there is "time and chance" (Ecc 9.11) while still affirming that the deeds of all are in God's hand (Ecc 9.1). Jim McGuiggan helpfully describes this concept of the sovereignty of God. Speaking about the

---

[15] N. Ward, *The Growth of the Seed*, 445. Further, it is striking, upon his freeing and promotion to grand vizier, he did not use his newfound power to visit his father and instead gave his firstborn a name that celebrated the ability to forget his father's household (Gen 41.51).

[16] Victor P. Hamilton, *The Book of Genesis: Chapters 18–50*, The New International Commentary on the Old Testament (Grand Rapids: Eerdmans, 1995), 575. It may be Joseph did not realize this even when the brothers came for the first time, depending on how the reader understands his request for Benjamin's attendance (is he only testing his brothers to see if they have changed or is he trying to rescue Benjamin from them, presuming they would sell him into Egypt as well?). It seems Judah's speech (Gen 44.18–34) is what crystalizes everything in Joseph's mind.

"Roman games" where Christians, including children, were fed to lions he writes,

> Say what we will about secondary agents and causes, say what we will about randomness and bad luck, say what we want about demonic powers and corrupted free will—say all of that and more, but when we're through, say that God was there accomplishing his will. No helpless watcher, wondering what he could do to squeeze some good out of it—he was an active participant![17]

How, then, does the modern Christian live in the light of such a powerful, but often seemingly-silent God?

First, there must be a regular appreciation of God's working in the world, especially as so much of the world tends toward secularism and even Christians tend toward deism. As Firth says, "God can work through the miraculous, but more often it is through something far simpler. We need, perhaps, to develop the skill of reflecting more on the seemingly ordinary events of life to appreciate how God has been at work in our daily experience."[18] Part of such a life is not only acknowledging God's activity, but seeing opportunities in it. Such providential working reflects "the importance of responding to the potentialities built into such providential positioning."[19] Just as the book of Esther "highlights the courage, the ingenuity, the wisdom of those Jews,"[20] so also modern Christians must take advantage of the providentially

---

[17] Jim McGuiggan, *Celebrating the Wrath of God: Reflections on the Agony and Ecstasy of His Relentless Love* (Colorado Springs: Waterbrook Press, 2001), 105.

[18] Firth, *The Message of Esther*, 99.

[19] Bruce C. Birch, et al. *A Theological Introduction to the Old Testament* 2nd ed. (Nashville: Abingdon Press, 2005), 453.

[20] V. Hamilton, *Handbook on the Historical Books*, 542. Hamilton goes on to say, "It is not the case that God is active (even if behind the scenes) while his people are passive."

placed moments in life. Christians must have eyes that are open to opportunities to work for the Lord, whether that be by teaching, by encouraging, by serving, or any other number of ministries.

Second, there must be a hesitance to speak for God. The reality is that without some kind of special revelation, people simply cannot know for certain what God is up to in their lives, and there should be humility in regard to this. There may be plausible guesses or, like Joseph, the benefit of decades' worth of hindsight may clarify God's working, but having certainty about God's working in the very moment is impossible and dangerously presumptuous. That great job offer, for example, may not have come from God's storehouses of blessing, but from Satan's bag of temptations—only time will tell. In Scripture, the great people of faith spoke much more hesitantly about God's dealings in their lives; "who knows" and "perhaps" were standard expressions. Their hesitancy does not detract from their faith. They clearly believed God was active, and he may well be working in that specific way, but they had the humility to allow for God to be sovereign—for his ways are unsearchable and unknowable (Isa 40.28; Psa 145.3; Rom 11.33; Eph 3.19–20; etc.)—and for him to reveal his purposes and plans on his own timeline.

It may be that God will reveal his purpose in a very short time. It may be 20 years or more before one finds out what God is doing. It may be, as in Job's case, that God never answers the "why" about various life events. Whatever may be the case, the biblical teaching is God is in control.[21] Just as Mordecai expressed uncertainty about God's working, the best human response is not to claim knowledge of God's working but to trust that he is and to let God be God.

---

[21] See N. Ward, *The Growth of the Seed*, 445–446.

# TEN

# *A Biblical Life in a Pagan World*

One question faced by the reader of Esther is what to think of the Jews who did not return from captivity, those who ultimately became "the Diaspora." In particular, at this early stage of development, does the book of Esther give us any clue as to how to understand them?

One perspective, represented by Dunne, is their remaining in Susa reflected a lack of desire for the homeland and is evidence of their assimilation into Persian culture, which is in contrast with the attitudes of the exiles who strongly desired a return (Jer 51.50; Psa 137.5–6).[1] Others, however, see their remaining as morally ambivalent at worst or perfectly acceptable at best. Jobes, for example, argues the book of Esther provides an affirmative answer to the question of whether the Jews of the Diaspora were still God's people in covenant relationship with

---

[1] Dunne, *Esther and Her Elusive God,* 19. Erich S. Gruen, *Diaspora: Jews Amidst Greeks and Romans* (Cambridge: Harvard University Press, 2002), 135 points out that they do not see themselves as victims: "The absence of express reflections, let alone lamentations, on the subject [of the circumstances of dwelling in scattered communities of the Mediterranean] suggests that diaspora was not a 'problem.' Nothing compelled the Jews to develop a theory of diaspora, whether as consolation or justification." See John M. G. Barclay, *Jews in the Mediterranean Diaspora: From Alexander to Trajan (323 BCE–117 CE)* (Oakland: University of California Press, 1999), 320–335 for a discussion of levels of assimilation among Diaspora Jews outside of Egypt.

him.[2] Ultimately, this question cannot be easily answered and the reader's decision will be guided by his or her own perspective on whether there was something inherently wrong with Diaspora Judaism. If there is nothing inherently wrong in it, it will be hard to fault Esther or Mordecai on the grounds that they did not return to Jerusalem; if Esther and Mordecai are faulted on those grounds, it will be hard to conclude anything other than Diaspora Judaism being fundamentally flawed. If it may be concluded that Diaspora Judaism itself is not inherently sinful, then the book of Esther provides a valuable picture of living in the midst of a pagan world. Indeed, to the modern Christian who has no physical Promised Land as an abiding residence, it may offer valuable insight into how one conducts himself or herself in a pagan culture.[3]

## A. Living Critically

David Firth argues that one of the values of the book of Esther is it gives a subtle, yet helpful model of dealing with the state. He says the book of Esther includes both the critical acceptance of some cultural and political traditions and the critical rejection of others, giving a pattern of how a God-fearing citizen can live according to his or her faith in an alien or oppressive context.[4] Firth first points to what has here been described as the satirical element of the story—Ahasuerus as a buffoon, the ex-

---

[2] Jobes, *Esther*, 42. Dunne, *Esther and Her Elusive God*, 4–5, by contrast, argues it shows God is steadfast and faithful even though the people do not deserve it.

[3] For more thorough studies on Diaspora Judaism particularly, see, e.g., Gruen, *Diaspora*,; Barclay, *Jews in the Mediterranean Diaspora*; John J. Collins, *Between Athens and Jerusalem: Jewish Identity in the Hellenistic Diaspora*, 2nd ed. (Grand Rapids: Eerdmans, 2000); etc.

[4] David G. Firth, "The Book of Esther: A Neglected Paradigm for Dealing with the State," *Old Testament Essays* 10 no. 1 (1997): 19.

travagant expense and waste of the parties and wife search, Haman's promotion and boasts, the irrevocable laws, the processes of government, etc.—as an illustration of the critical rejection of the state. He argues that, although nothing is said directly, it is clear "the system of government has lost all touch with reality." [5] More significantly, he argues the author has an understanding of kingship rooted in Deuteronomy 17.14–20, which shapes the perspective of what is expected of a ruler—a blueprint from which Ahasuerus deviates at nearly every point—thus providing a "strong, though inferential" case that part of the author's purpose is to define what the state should be. [6]

On the other hand, there are some elements of the governmental system that are critically accepted. Esther functions within the royal court system to achieve the aim of delivering her people. Mordecai also plays an active role in the state, going so far as to save the king's life and receive public honor from the grand vizier for having done so. It seems clear, as Firth says, they use those elements of the system that function for the good of the people. This, he argues, is not a wholesale adoption or acceptance of the system, but "a process of critical acceptance of those elements that allowed them to live as the people of God" (cf. Rom 13.1–7; 1 Pet 2.13–17). [7]

## B. Seek the Peace

More than 100 years before Ahasuerus took the throne of Persia, Jeremiah wrote a letter to the exiles in Babylonian cap-

---

[5] Ibid, 21.

[6] Ibid., 22. Given the author's constant interaction with other Old Testament narratives (see chapter 4, above), it is no stretch to argue for such a contrast between Ahasuerus and the Deuteronomy standard.

[7] Ibid., 24.

tivity (Jer 29). To the average Jew who heard Hananiah's false prophecies about a brief captivity (Jer 28.2–4), who boasted in the Temple as a reason for security (Jer 7.4), or who simply believed Jews were superior to unclean Gentiles, Jeremiah's letter was, at best, counterintuitive. The basic message was to settle down and prepare to live a long life in captivity. Perhaps more shocking than that was the directive to "seek the welfare of the city" (Jer 29.7). In that light, Humphreys argues Esther (and Daniel) affirm the possibility of living a creative and rich life in the Diaspora "as a part of the complex social, political, and economic dynamics of the world, and also of remaining a devoted and loyal member of his community of fellow Jews."[8] Humphreys suggests the life of full interaction with a pagan environment, as seen in Esther, could result in hostility toward Jews because of one's Jewishness but could be overcome through the very same interaction.[9] The basic principle of Jeremiah's letter, then, was to recognize the interdependence of the Jewish community and its host environment.[10]

Although Humphreys does not emphasize this, it is also clear that Mordecai and Esther are seeking the good of the city in their deeds themselves. Mordecai's discovery and prevention of the assassination plot against Ahasuerus fits squarely under this heading. Given Haman's egotism, the citizens' and palace staff's apparent feelings for him,[11] and the populace's reaction to the decree calling for the extermination of the Jews, it could also be argued that deposing Haman and saving the Jewish people

---

[8] W. Lee Humphreys, "A Life-Style for Diaspora: A Study of the Tales of Esther and Daniel," *Journal of Biblical Literature* 92 no. 2 (1973): 216.

[9] Ibid., 222–223.

[10] Webb, *Five Festal Garments*, 118.

[11] See pages 84–86, above.

is itself a working of good for the city.[12] This may be further strengthened by the populace's identification with the Jews upon the release of the second decree. Finally, the authority wielded by Mordecai after his promotion should be understood as being for the benefit of the people. While the final detailing of the benefits of his authority is Jew-centered (10.3), the widespread celebration at his advancement (8.15) speaks to his universal popularity among those who knew him. Since he was situated at the gate of the city, he likely would have been well known in the city, and the celebration should not be understood as only by Jews[13] but by all who knew him. Indeed, it may well have been the knowledge of Mordecai and his character that led to such celebration. It is no stretch, then, to suggest Mordecai continued to seek the good of all people, not merely the Jews who are specifically highlighted in chapter 10.[14]

## C. Application

Firth says that inasmuch as the government may work against the good of the people, it should be rejected—though the people of God may work within the system for the good of the same people. He concludes that the Jews in the book of Esther, as the people of God, are called to "a practice of critical engagement as they deal with the existence of a foreign, and even oppressive,

---

[12] If the Jews of the Diaspora fulfilled their mission of being a light to the nations (Isa 42.6; 49.6), then their preservation was certainly for the good of the city around them. Even without this spiritual application, it is not hard to see how the people would have seen this as an improvement.

[13] Levenson, *Esther*, 116.

[14] But see Weisman, *Political Satire in the Bible*, 157 for an argument that Mordecai had inherited not only Haman's high status in the royal court, but also something of his domineering ways, and that the praise of Mordecai in chapter 10 is "diluted with a touch of satire."

government."[15] The application of this point is not difficult to see. In a government that increasingly separates itself from all things religious and becomes increasingly hostile to traditional Christian values, a Christian today must have the same circumspection and act accordingly. We must allow room for a critical interaction with the government that works within and through the system as possible to provide for the good of God's people without a wholesale endorsement of what that government itself stands for.[16] That this is possible may be further seen in Paul's endorsement of Nero's Roman Empire as being authorized by God (Rom 13.1–7; cf. 1 Pet 2.13–17)—a shocking matter, given the decadence and anti-Christian stance of Nero's Rome.[17]

Likewise, as Esther and Mordecai did, Christians must seek the welfare of the cities and nations in which they live.[18] Just as Jeremiah instructed the Judean exiles, the Christian's purpose is to "start salting our city with acts of grace that spring from hearts overflowing with compassion."[19] Although there are always exceptions, "we as a people have largely abdicated goodness to formless, faceless government welfare programs and

---

[15] David Firth, "The Book of Esther: A Neglected Paradigm," 24.

[16] This point is not intended to suggest morality can be imposed by legislation or that Jesus' kingdom is to be of this world. While the New Testament teaching is clearly counter-cultural, neither Christ nor his apostles sought to achieve success through government edict but by individual conversion, which should be the goal and purpose of Christians today, as well.

[17] See, e.g., Everett Ferguson, *Backgrounds of Early Christianity*, 3rd ed. (Grand Rapids: Eerdmans, 2003), 33–35 for a helpful summary of Nero's Rome.

[18] Gruen, *Diaspora*, 135 calls Jeremiah's letter "a blueprint for diaspora existence, a guide for Jews who were developing strategies for survival and success in lands governed by Gentiles." If modern Christians are indeed in a similar situation to Diaspora Jews, then it is also a manifesto for today.

[19] Keith Ward, "Seek the Welfare of the City," *Living in Captivity: God's People in a Time of Crisis,* Florida College Annual Lectures (Temple Terrace: FC Press, 2010), 182.

organized charities." [20] By contrast, Christians should shower the people around them with Christ's love through individual service to the point that they want to share in it, following after the pattern of Jesus. Ward concludes, "When God walked, he went where people hurt and he healed; when God talked, he spoke words of comfort and hope; when God relaxed, he played with the children. He went to weddings and to funerals, to feasts, and to quiet places with a few." [21] As Jesus was among the people—even and especially the downhearted and rejected—so Christians are called to be in their communities.

The Book of Esther may also suggest that this life of critical interaction and peace seeking in a pagan world may be fraught with danger. Since the Fall, there has been enmity between the seed of the woman and the seed of the serpent, [22] which plays itself out through the rest of Genesis and the Bible. In Esther, Haman's accusation against the Jews is rooted in their particularity as unassimilated, and their following a different law is highlighted as an especially heinous crime (Est 3.8). As Webb suggests, the scandal of particularity remains, as the elect remain strangers of the dispersion, though it is now rooted in identifying with Christ rather than identifying with the Law of Moses. [23] Since the way of Christ is, at best, foolishness to the world (1 Cor 1.18–25), the Christian should not be surprised the world continues to hate him or her: God's people always have been, and always will be, the objects of hatred and contempt.

---

[20] Ibid.

[21] Ibid., 183.

[22] See N. Ward, *The Growth of the Seed*, 66–67 for an argument that this refers to conflict between those who follow God and those who follow Satan (cf. John 8.41–42; 1 John 3.8) rather than humans and snakes.

[23] Webb, *Five Festal Garments*, 131.

Haman is an embodiment of this hatred and reminds the reader that even when the opposition seems insurmountable, even in the absences of miracles, God remains sovereign and present. As Webb points out, this belief is not to whistle in the dark but to remember that even when God seems most absent, nothing can ultimately thwart his purposes.[24]

### D. Conclusion

This concluding section examined the character development of Esther, the "who knows" statement of Mordecai in its interbiblical context, and Mordecai's and Esther's interaction with the state. The purpose is to argue that the silent but providential nature of God's dealings with his people in the book of Esther can teach a variety of lessons to the reader. Among these are the need for individual growth through character development that results in actively working for the good of God's people. At the same time, believers need faith in God's dealings with mankind, yet a respect for the sovereignty of God that does not presume upon him. Finally, God's people must deal with the pagan culture in which they live: Christians should have thoughtful circumspection in dealing with the state—rejecting some things while accepting and using others that are beneficial. In this way, Christians will, as Jeremiah instructed the exiles, seek the peace of the city.

The book of Esther, though it displays no overt traits of the Jewish religion, can be shown to be religious through a series of interbiblical references that run through the course of the narrative. This establishes the framework to see the coincidences—particularly those at the pivot of the narrative in

---

[24] Ibid., 132–133.

Esther 6—as well as the literary clues and other subtle hints in the same religious light. As a result, the Christian minister should not be afraid to teach from it, seeking to show lessons such as, but not at all limited to, those in this book. Doing so may well reintroduce a marvelous story and its lessons to a generation of Christians who have nearly forgotten this re-markable book of the Bible.

# *Exegesis of Esther 6*

Having established the religious and providential nature of Esther, I will now interpret what is universally agreed upon as the most significant chapter in the book of Esther.[1]

## A. Exegesis of Esther 6

Earlier, I argued for the literary and thematic centrality of chapter 6 within the Esther narrative; now, we turn to an interpretation of that chapter, to show God's implied presence throughout. This interpretative premise is guided by the principles discussed in the previous chapter that give Esther a religious context, primarily the interbiblical nature of the book of Esther.

### 1. Context

After Haman's decree, Mordecai convinces Esther to plead for her people. At her first meeting with Ahasuerus, she invites him and Haman to a feast she had already prepared. At that feast, she postpones making her request until a second feast. Haman is jubilant to have been a special guest at each of Es-

---

[1] Because the focus my D.Min. was theological exegesis, the major project included an exegetical section. I chose Esther 6 as my text due to its significance in the overall structure of Esther. Although a lengthy exegesis seemed out of place in the context of the chapters of this book, I wanted to include it as an appendix for those who might find an exegesis of this central chapter to be helpful.

ther's feasts, but his psyche is fragile.[2] Upon seeing Mordecai, who still does not show him respect or fear, he is undone.[3] He goes home and enumerates his great blessings and accomplishments in front of the people who would know them best, ultimately advertising to them "the fact that one uncooperative underling can outweigh these accomplishments. The balloon swells and swells and finally pops with the application of one small pin."[4]

Haman's wife, Zeresh, advises him to use his authority to have Mordecai executed: "Let a gallows fifty cubits high be made, and in the morning tell the king to have Mordecai hanged upon it. Then go joyfully with the king to the feast" (Est 5.14).[5] Zeresh plays to Haman's ego in two ways: first, she suggests giant-sized vengeance for his giant-sized ego;[6] second, she instructs Haman to "tell" the king to have Mordecai hanged on it. As Bechtel says, "Either these people are familiar with Haman's tendency to think more highly of himself than he ought to think, or they

---

[2] Duguid, *Esther and Ruth*, 65 points out that this reveals how Haman's entire world revolved around his ego: "When it was stroked ... he felt blessed, even though nothing in the real world had actually changed. His power had not actually increased, yet Haman rejoiced. Likewise, his power was not really diminished by Mordecai's refusal to bow, yet Haman was incensed by it."

[3] Laniak, "Esther," 234 says, "How ironic that the queen's flattering invitation was in reality a greater threat than Mordecai's indifference."

[4] Bechtel, *Esther*, 55.

[5] Jobes, *Esther*, 146 notes a further irony here: as he follows the advice of his wife, he is not following the edict of Esther 1 that "every man should be ruler over his own household" (1.22).

[6] Duguid, *Esther and Ruth*, 67 points out an ironic problem with this proposed solution: "[T]he very size of the gallows would have unintentionally elevated Mordecai to a position of significance: his very death would have drawn all eyes to him (and away from Haman) in a way that a smaller gallows would not have done."

share in his presumption and over-confidence."[7] The irony here is, of course, that had Haman simply waited for the decree to take effect, Mordecai would have eventually been disposed of, and Haman would have never experienced the humiliation of chapter 6. Instead, because his pride would not allow for Mordecai to live another day, he finds himself humiliated and, in the end, executed in Mordecai's place, a stake of his own devising.[8]

Due to Haman's plan, it is evident from the outset that there is going to be tension in this chapter: at the end of chapter 5, Haman begins plotting Mordecai's death; at the beginning of chapter 6, Ahasuerus begins planning to honor him. Although the reader is not sure how the tension will resolve itself as the chapter begins, Ahasuerus and Haman ultimately meet in what is one of the most comical scenes in the Bible. What leads to the comedy are the multiple silences that run throughout. Fox says,

> The name of the honoree is not mentioned until after Haman describes the honors; the fact that the honoree is Haman's enemy and the king's benefactor is unknown to Haman; the conflict between Haman and Mordecai is unknown to Xerxes; and Haman maintains silence about his personal enmity toward Mordecai. ... [T]he farcical quality of the scene derives from these disjointed silences and misapprehensions, with each party speaking out of a conflicting set of assumptions and at cross-purposes.[9]

---

[7] Bechtel, *Esther*, 55–56.

[8] Laniak, "Esther," 235 points out Haman has now concocted two plans that will backfire: "The date that was set to witness the widespread destruction of the Jews will become the day for executing those who hate the Jews. This gallows, intended to single out Mordecai as the first among those executed for *being* Jews, will make Haman first among those executed for *opposing* Jews."

[9] Fox, *Character and Ideology*, 78.

## 2. *Sleepless in Susa* (6.1–5)[10]

Having set the context, we now turn to the interpretation of the chapter. As this chapter begins, King Ahasuerus cannot sleep, which leads to a series of bizarre and extreme coincidences.[11] Before the chapter is complete, Haman will be forced to honor Mordecai with the very ceremony he believed to be designing for himself, which will be but a foretaste of his receipt of the evil he had intended for the Jews. As already noted, Haman's request would render Esther's unfolding plan useless for Mordecai—and all seems to be going in Haman's favor: his last task is to get the king's approval for Mordecai's execution. Since the king has not yet refused a recommendation or request, this would seem an easy approval to get.[12] Further, if the king can be manipulated to consent to the annihilation of a people, it should be quite simple to gain his consent to the elimination of one man.[13] Because Esther does not know about Haman's plans, she cannot intervene on behalf of Mordecai before the second banquet; unless someone or something else intervenes, Mordecai will be dead before Esther sees Ahasuerus again and thus "ineligible" for the reprieve Esther will ask for.[14]

**6.1,** *On that night the king could not sleep.* Literally, this says "the king's sleep had fled."[15] The cause is not given and speculation abounds. Phillips suggests it could have been related to

---

[10] Section heading taken from Duguid, *Esther and Ruth*, 74.

[11] Since they are discussed in some detail above, they will not be recounted again here.

[12] Beal, "Esther," 78.

[13] Bush, *Ruth, Esther*, 418.

[14] Bechtel, *Esther*, 57.

[15] Many ancient versions "corrected" this by saying God took it from him. See Paton, 244 for a listing.

Esther's impending request[16] or Haman's attendance at her banquets.[17] Levenson, on the other hand, suggests it may be one of the many "unmotivated events" in Esther, such as Vashti's refusal, Esther's winning favor, and Mordecai's refusal to bow, saying, "Actions seem to come out of nowhere in this tale, but they gradually link together to form an immensely positive and meaningful pattern of Jewish deliverance."[18]

The king's insomnia itself may be a hint at providential working for, as Whitcomb says, "God accomplishes some of his deepest work in the hearts of men as they lay awake on their beds at night (cf. Job 4.12–16; Ps 4.4; Acts 18.9; 23.11)."[19] This is likely how a Jewish audience would have read it,[20] and it remained a prevailing view. Jerome, for example, argues that being reminded of Mordecai the Jew's good deed would lay the groundwork for Esther's acceptability when she reveals her ethnic identity so all the Jewish people would escape imminent death.[21]

---

[16] See Anthony Tomasino, *Esther*, Evangelical Exegetical Commentary (Bellingham: Lexham Press), 2003, *ad loc.* for a discussion of this perspective.

[17] Phillips, "Esther," 642. Talmud Megillah 15b says Ahasuerus' insomnia is due to Esther's invitations of Haman to the feasts and the thought they might conspire against him to kill him, which directly leads to his request for the chronicles to be read. Beal, "Esther," 79–80 suggests that, if this is the case, it might explain why the section regarding the last palace coup was read.

[18] Levenson, *Esther*, 95.

[19] Whitcomb, *Esther*, 87. Huey, "Esther," 821 says, "It would be futile to speculate on the cause of the king's sleeplessness, but we can be sure that God was behind it." Cf. Cohen, *Megilath Esther*, 53 who points back to the Rabbis who see this as evidence of God's intervention rather than mere coincidence.

[20] V.H. Matthews, M.W. Chavalas, and J.H. Walton, *The IVP Bible Background Commentary: Old Testament*, electronic ed. (Downers Grove, IL: InterVarsity Press, 2000), *ad loc.*

[21] Marco Conti, *1–2 Kings, 1–2 Chronicles, Ezra, Nehemiah, Esther*, Ancient Christian Commentary on Scripture (Downers Grove: Inter-Varsity Press, 2008), 388.

Reid points out that "that night" parallels with "that day" in 5.9, emphasizing the closely related timing. Previously in the narrative, time moved very quickly—years passing by in a matter of verses—but, now, at the heart of the story, the passing of time is slowed down as every detail of the event is recalled, indicating the centrality of these chapters in the overall scheme of the story.[22]

*And he gave orders to bring the book of memorable deeds, the chronicles....* The king's motivation for having the chronicles read to him is not given. Wells is astonished that a king with an irresistible wife and a line of concubines long enough to see them nightly should "choose as his nocturnal entertainment highlights from the annals of the kings of Persia,"[23] which may be part of the remarkable "coincidence" at work. At the very least, in the king's mind, it is a way of passing time that would allow him to review recent history with himself cast in the best possible light.[24] On the other hand, it may be part of the satire of the story, as mentioned in chapter 5.[25]

---

[22] Reid, *Esther,* 116.

[23] Wells, "Esther," 65.

[24] Laniak, "Esther," 238.

[25] Firth, *The Message of Esther,* 92 says, "Many a Christian who was perhaps a little weary at the time has found how hard it can be to stay awake during a dull sermon, and since the Chronicles of the kingdom were probably a rather boring book, rather like an extended journal of the king's daily experiences, it is easy to imagine that having it read would be somewhat soporific. So, we are probably to imagine that the king is listening to the reading of the Chronicle with the sole goal of being put to sleep." Tomasino, *Esther, ad loc.* adds, "What could have been more monotonous than the royal archives?" If this interpretation has any merit, the notion that a king would implicitly call his own history boring is likely to be seen as satire, especially considering the clear satire that pervades so much of the narrative.

*They were read before the king.* The periphrastic form of the verb in the Hebrew suggests a lengthy reading,[26] which might lend credence to the soporific effect it would have had.

**6.2,** *And it was found written how Mordecai had told about Bigthana and Teresh, two of the king's eunuchs, who guarded the threshold, and who had sought to lay hands on King Ahasuerus.* Beal suggests a certain suspense as the annals are reread, since it is not clear in 2.23 which details of the event were recorded—the astute reader knows the Jews need a lifeline, and this may well be it, but only if Mordecai is named; "As it turns out, Mordecai's name *had* been included in the written report."[27]

This scene also begins to unravel the answer to a question that has stood in tension since chapter 3: which of the two royal documents concerning Mordecai—one that identifies him as a friend and protector of the king; the other that identifies him and his people for annihilation—would stand?[28]

**6.3,** *And the king said, "What honor or distinction has been bestowed on Mordecai for this?"* In the Persian world, bestowing honor was a significant matter, as honor and shame repeatedly function as core values for the culture, which is clear at the outset of the Esther story: the king has dismissed Queen Vashti because she brought shame on him, and Haman's rage at Mordecai is prompted by the latter's refusal to honor him.[29] Further, it was

---

[26] Clines, *Ezra, Nehemiah, Esther,* 307; cf. Keil, "Esther," 223. Philips, "Esther," 643, adds, "The court reader(s) may have been droning on for a good part of the night."

[27] Beal, "Esther," 80. This does not, however, solve the problem of the king not knowing the Jews are the ethnic group destined for destruction. See comments on verse 10, below.

[28] Beal, "Esther," 84.

[29] Eugene F. Roop, *Ruth, Jonah, Esther,* Believers Church Bible Commentary (Scottdale: Herald Press, 2002), 220.

a matter of honor with Persian kings to reward their benefactors quickly and magnificently,[30] though this was as much an opportunity to display the king's generosity as it was to reward the individual.[31] The "honor" and "distinction" that should have been Mordecai's upon his uncovering the plot (2.19–23) went to Haman instead (3.1–2).[32]

*The king's young men who attended him said, "Nothing has been done for him."* The servants, like the young men in 2.2–4, the servants in 3.3–5, and Harbona in 7.9–10, "possess a great deal of knowledge/power as mediators of information. … [E]verything depends on the servants as mediators. If they lie and say that something has been done for Mordecai, the king would pass over this story from the annals and move on to the next without further comment."[33]

Due to Persia's shame/honor culture and the king's standing policy of swiftly rewarding benefactors, this oversight was potentially catastrophic. An honorable deed not properly recognized put the honor of both subject and sovereign at risk, which now put the king in a bind. Ahasuerus' quandary was to find a way to restore his own honor by publicly restoring his benefactor's as public focus was not only directed toward the good deed but toward the appropriate honor considered commensurate with the benefaction; it was not sufficient that

---

[30] Paton, *Esther*, 245.

[31] Reid, *Esther*, 117.

[32] The appearance of Haman's name as the object of Ahasuerus' promotion is a jarring moment in the narrative following Mordecai's provision of life-saving intelligence. Some commentators suggest the perceived slight is the motivation for Mordecai's refusal to bow.

[33] Beal, "Esther," 80. Beal also points to a certain irony in this statement, "since Haman is now seeking to do something radically *dishonorable* with him even as they speak. Yet Haman has done nothing with him either, as of yet."

honors be merely given, but that honors were seen by all to have been given.[34]

**6.4,** *And the king said, "Who is in the court?"* As noted in the chapter 5, Ahasuerus is helpless without his advisors. Duguid appropriately paraphrases this question, "[W]hich of my counselors is around to tell me what to do?"[35] Since Ahasuerus' question presumes someone would be around, it is likely that Haman has not arrived before normal working hours.[36] Although some see Haman arriving in the middle of the night,[37] he was likely as occupied preparing the stake for Mordecai's impending execution as Ahasuerus was listening to the annals being read. Further, Tomasino points to Zeresh's instructions to go to the king in the morning (5.14) and Ahasuerus' instructions for Haman to immediately carry out his instructions (6.10) as evidence that Ahasuerus listened to the chronicles read all night and that Haman arrived early the next day to make his request.[38]

*Now Haman had just entered the outer court of the king's palace to speak to the king about having Mordecai hanged on the gallows that he had prepared for him.* Like Ahasuerus, thoughts of Mordecai have kept Haman from sleeping, as well. They meet here as each of them are eager to solve their respective problems: "Haman must kill and humiliate Mordecai, or he can have no peace of mind; and King [Ahasuerus] must honor Mordecai, or his sleepless nights will continue."[39] Firth says the phrasing

---

[34] Laniak, *Shame and Honor,* 105.

[35] Duguid, *Esther and Ruth,* 76.

[36] Fox, *Character and Ideology,* 76. Cf. Keil, "Esther," 225; Paton, *Esther,* 244.

[37] E.g., Huey, "Esther," 822; Berlin, *Esther,* 58; Bush, *Ruth, Esther,* 419.

[38] Tomasino, *Esther,* 6.1.

[39] Ibid., *ad loc.*

here suggests Haman arrived just as the king is asking who is present: "at exactly the right moment to solve the king's dilemma, but in such a way as to trap himself. ...The timing is perfect."[40]

**6.5,** *And the king's young men told him, "Haman is there, standing in the court."* One of the greatest ironies of the chapter is that, when any adviser would have served the king's purpose, "it is Haman who must give advice on how Mordecai should be honored, and moreover, that he should be in the position to give that advice only because he is early at the palace to get authorization for Mordecai's execution."[41] Part of what makes it so ironic is his timing would seem serendipitous to the young men and the king as well, though for a decidedly different reason. From their perspective, nothing could be better than to have the leading official present at precisely the time the king needs him.[42]

The opening word in Hebrew is הִנֵּה, which the ESV unfortunately translates as "there" ("Haman is there"), rather than as "Look!" or "Behold!" which is the more standard meaning.[43] Although הִנֵּה is a common word in the Old Testament, Beal points out that it is only used two other times in Esther. In each other instance it draws attention to speech concerning the downfall of Haman and the corresponding rise of Esther

---

[40] Firth, *The Message of Esther,* 93–94.

[41] Clines, *Ezra, Nehemiah, Esther,* 307. Moore, 64 is frequently quoted here, and for obvious reason: "Here, the early bird is gotten by the worm."

[42] Firth, *The Message of Esther,* 94.

[43] Francis Brown, Samuel Rolles Driver, and Charles Augustus Briggs, *Enhanced Brown-Driver-Briggs Hebrew and English Lexicon* (Oak Harbor, WA: Logos Research Systems, 2000), 243.

and Mordecai.[44] If that is intended to be a recurring theme in relation to this word, its use here also points to the imminent turn of events.

*And the king said, "Let him come in."* In addition to his over-active ego, Haman's presumption of his own impending honor "may also be inspired by what must seem like a fortuitous invitation into the king's chamber in the early morning, at the very moment he was so eager for an audience."[45] Haman must feel, at the moment, like he is unstoppable—invitations from the queen, great advice from his wife, his nemesis about to die once he gets to ask a simple question, the king immediately inviting him in. What could possibly go wrong?

### 3. *Delusions of Grandeur* (6.6–9)[46]

Here, we encounter dramatic irony—the audience knows what the characters do not: "a meeting of persons but not of minds."[47] Further, as Ahasuerus and Haman have this conversation, there is irony built into what had been happening to each of them the previous night and the conflicting intentions of each.[48] It is intended to be read as comedy—a bit like Abbot and Costello having a conversation that only the audience understands.[49] Haman had arrived early that day to ask for Mordecai's neck; Ahasuerus was sleepless all night and now wants to honor Mordecai. One of the great ironies of the Esther story is that Haman is to

---

[44] Beal, "Esther," 81. Cf. 7.9; 8.7.

[45] Fox, *Character and Ideology*, 76.

[46] This section heading is probably apparent enough not to need citation, but I first saw it in Bechtel, 58.

[47] Baldwin, *Esther*, 90.

[48] Ibid.

[49] Bechtel, *Esther*, 59.

decide how to honor the man he desired to hang.[50] A further irony is that if Haman had not been so anxious to get the king's permission to kill Mordecai, he would never have been on hand for his own humiliation.[51]

This scene also reveals just how important prestige is to Haman: he could have asked for anything (at least, according to his incorrect assumption that the king is speaking about him), but what he wanted was to dress up in the king's clothes and ride around on the king's horse with a herald telling everyone the king is honoring him. Beal says, "At this royal offer, as he interprets it, Haman's self-aggrandizing fantasies run wild, and he imagines nothing less than masquerading as king in the most public way."[52] If Ahasuerus sees through Haman's thinly-veiled ego, this request would likely have aroused in him great suspicion about Haman's ambitions. After all, to wear the king's robes and ride the king's horse was tantamount to being another king.[53] Haman's royal fetish is made clear by his eightfold description of the ceremony as "royal" (מַלְכוּת) or use of the term "king" (מֶלֶךְ). In his mind, there is a clear equation between honor and royalty that only being king would satisfy.[54]

**6.6,** *So Haman came in, and the king said to him...* While it is natural that the king would speak first in this situation any-

---

[50] Huey, "Esther," 823.

[51] Bechtel, *Esther,* 58.

[52] Beal, "Esther," 82.

[53] McConville, *Ezra, Nehemiah, and Esther,* 179. Wells, "Esther," 67 says, "What he is describing is a coronation." J.M. Sasson, "Esther," *The Literary Guide to the Bible,* ed. Robert Alter and Frank Kermode (Cambridge: Belknap Press, 1987), 341 points to cuneiform evidence that suggests he is proposing treatment reserved for substitute kings.

[54] Laniak, "Esther," 239. See pages 62–63 for a contrast of this scene with the honoring of Joseph in Genesis 41.

way, it is vital to Mordecai's life that Ahasuerus be allowed to speak before Haman. Even with the king intent on honoring Mordecai, he is so easily swayed by advisors that a single word from Haman could have undone his plans to honor him; we could find Mordecai on a stake if Haman were allowed to speak first. Instead, not only does Ahasuerus speak first, but Haman is dismissed before he is able to present his concern because the business of remedying the king's dishonor takes precedence over all other matters.[55]

*"What should be done to the man whom the king delights to honor?"* While the reader may initially be dismayed over the king asking Haman for the proper way to honor Mordecai,[56] it is a further irony that he unintentionally does the same to Haman that Haman had done to him in Esther 3: withholding the name of the man he wishes to honor even as Haman had intentionally kept the name of the people he wished to destroy.[57] It is also significant that Ahasuerus changed his wording from "recognition" (גְּדוּלָּה), which he had said before Haman arrived in verse 3. As an already-promoted man, Haman might have presumed Ahasuerus did not mean him if he had again used the term "recognition" here.[58]

*And Haman said to himself, "Whom would the king delight to honor more than me?"* Aside from his own distended ego and the king's early-morning invitation, Laniak summarizes well the situation that would lead to this line of thought:

---

[55] Tomasino, *Esther*, *ad loc.*

[56] Moore, *Esther*, 67.

[57] Clines, *Ezra, Nehemiah, Esther*, 307.

[58] Reid, *Esther*, 118. Reid also raises the possibility that Ahasuerus is setting Haman up. While, as she mentions, it would provide "an interesting angle on Haman and Xerxes' relationship," it probably attributes too much adeptness to a king who is cast as a buffoon.

Had not the line between his own wishes and the king's command become quite permeable in chapter 3? Wasn't the king, of late, quite magnanimous when the queen had approached unbidden? Didn't the *exclusive* guest list for the queen's banquets suggest a shared admiration for him by the royal couple? And now he finds the king waiting for him early in the morning with what appears to be a blank check![59]

This glimpse into his inner thoughts bares Haman's soul for all to see. Ultimately, all he cares about—even more than revenge against his chief foe—is his own honor. Honor is his lifeblood; the one thing that will divert him from even his plan against Mordecai is the thought of honor.[60] Here, Haman sees only the possibility of reward for himself. For someone whose ego is as inflated as Haman's, there is nothing more desirable than glory and honor.[61] It is also significant that Haman is so convinced he is the honoree, he does not think to ask who the king might be talking about. It never crosses Haman's mind that it could be anyone other than him. Yet if Haman had simply asked whom the king had in mind, his answer would have certainly differed, and the whole story would have changed.[62] In that case, the dismay Moore suggests the reader might initially have would be well founded.

**6.7,** *And Haman said to the king....* Haman's quick answer may suggest he had long thought about this very possibility and was thus ready to give the response if the king ever asked.[63] Fur-

---

[59] Laniak, "Esther," 238.

[60] Clines, *Ezra, Nehemiah, Esther,* 307–308. But see comment on verse 9 below; Mordecai may have still been at least in the back of his mind.

[61] Firth, *The Message of Esther,* 95.

[62] Ibid.

[63] Whitcomb, *Esther,* 89.

ther, the syntax of the sentence is disjointed,[64] revealing Haman's overanxiousness to promote himself.[65] At the point in his answer when it would have been appropriate to show formal deference to the king (cf. 5.4, 7–8), he eagerly seeks to take advantage of the situation to his own greedy ends.[66] Berlin contrasts this with Esther's response. Unlike Esther, Haman does not speak in the formal language of an inferior addressing a superior. He gets right to the point, as if speaking to an equal, suggesting an implication to which most royalty would not take kindly.[67]

*"For the man whom the king delights to honor..."* Haman begins a sentence but breaks off before completing it, suggesting that he is pausing to savor the phrase.[68] Fox also notes that the broken syntax in the Hebrew "suggests a pause in which Haman hastily cogitates on how he should exploit his unexpected opportunity."[69] And Haman returns to this phrase, a leitmotif in this scene. Fox points out that he "rolls the phrase ... around in his mouth four times, beginning and ending his little speech with it," but Haman will ultimately have to repeatedly proclaim it about Mordecai. Fox concludes, "It is easy to imagine how the words Haman once savored will then fill his mouth with gall."[70]

---

[64] This is best taken as anacoluthon. Cf. Bush, *Ruth, Esther,* 414; Keil, "Esther," 226; Tomasino, *Esther, ad loc.*

[65] Bush, *Ruth, Esther,* 415 says, "By the anacoluthon [the narrator] implies that Haman is so eager to answer the king ... that he begins the sentence with that which is foremost in his thoughts, 'the man whom the king wishes to honor,' since he is so sure that this refers to himself. Then, he must break off the sense and begin again in order to describe the honor he wishes to have."

[66] Laniak, *Shame and Honor,* 100. Bush, 415 points to this "unseemly haste" as another way the narrator depicts Haman with subtle irony.

[67] Berlin, *Esther,* 58.

[68] Fox, *Character and Ideology,* 76.

[69] Ibid., 75n46.

[70] Ibid., 76

**6.8,** *"Let royal robes be brought, which the king has worn."* It is striking that Haman does not mention wealth or power, the sort of reward many would have wanted if given a blank check by the most powerful king in the world. It cannot be merely that he already has wealth and power for he already has honor and recognition, as well. In this we see a clear picture of Haman's character and priorities: his appetite for honor and recognition is insatiable.[71]

The Persian king's robe is described by Xenophon as purple with gold embroidery. Plutarch also reports that Artaxerxes once honored a request for his royal robe but qualified the gift with the command that it not be worn.[72] Jobes says there is some evidence that the Persian royal robes were believed to have "the power to impart the benefits of royalty in an almost magical way."[73] Berlin adds, "A person's garment is considered a part of his body, or a part of his being," and goes on to cite a variety of Old Testament passages that give context to Haman's request.[74] Even if all (or any) of these are not in Haman's mind, wearing the king's clothes certainly would put one in close contact with the king.

*"And the horse that the king has ridden."* Laniak points out that Solomon's ride on David's mule (1 Kgs 1.33) is a public ceremony of succession,[75] and Haman may have wished to give the impression that Ahasuerus had marked Haman as his succes-

---

[71] Ibid.

[72] Matthews, et al., *The IVP Bible Background Commentary: Old Testament*, Es 6.7.

[73] Jobes, *Esther*, 153. Cf. Fox, *Character and Ideology*, 77.

[74] Berlin, *Esther*, 59. Cf. Deuteronomy 14.1–2; 2 Samuel 10.4–5; 2 Kings 9.13; Numbers 20.25–28; 1 Samuel 24.

[75] Laniak, *Shame and Honor*, 101.

sor.[76] Also, multiple commentators argue that putting on the royal robe is the first act of any usurper.[77]

*"And on whose head a royal crown is set."* Most interpreters understand this as either referring to the headdress Persian horses may have worn[78] or to mean the horse that the king, wearing his royal crown, rode.[79] Bush, however, says the syntax is clear and unmistakable: the crown is on the head of the horse.[80] Tomasino probably offers the best solution, arguing, "whether the practice is attested elsewhere is largely irrelevant. It clearly signifies Haman's obsession with kingship."[81]

**6.9,** *"And let the robes and the horse be handed over to one of the king's most noble officials."* To be led by the most noble official would ensure everyone sees Haman's high position of honor, as it would demonstrate he was superior in the king's regard to even his greatest officials.[82] Haman's mistake, of course, is he unwittingly makes his own rank a qualification for the role that will humiliate him.[83]

---

[76] Cf. Mark Mangano, *Esther and Daniel*, The College Press NIV Commentary (Joplin: College Press: 2001), 91.

[77] E.g., Phillips, "Esther," 644 says, "Haman's comments could be construed as the first step in a plan to usurp the throne."

[78] Phillips, "Esther," 645 points to stone reliefs from Nineveh that show Assyrian horses wearing some form of headdress, which continued into the Persian Period, as demonstrated from reliefs in Persepolis. Firth, *The Message of Esther*, 96 says, "If so, the horse's headdress may be a means of indicating that this is a royal horse, somewhat akin to the flags placed on the cars of heads of state in motorcades."

[79] E.g., Clines, *Ezra, Nehemiah, Esther*, 308. A complete different view is that of Roop, *Ruth, Jonah, Esther*, 220, who instead sees it as a comedic element: "A man's craving for honor causes him to get everything wrong."

[80] Bush, *Ruth, Esther*, 415. Cf. Paton, *Esther*, 248.

[81] Tomasino, *Esther, ad loc.*

[82] Ibid.

[83] Fox, *Character and Ideology*, 77.

*"Let them dress the man whom the king delights to honor, and let them lead him on the horse through the square of the city."* It is no accident Haman plans his parade route through the city square, which was the center of the city's activity and the location of the most important men in the city: "Haman's parade would process through the populous plaza of the city, so that everyone would see the extent of his honor. This was his dream day."[84] More specifically, as Reid points out, Haman is planning his finest moment to take place directly in front of Mordecai as he sat in front of the king's gate; it appears the old enmity has not been forgotten amid his present enthusiasm after all: "The thought of Mordecai embitters even the best moments of his life, and every moment is an opportunity to score a proverbial point."[85]

*"Proclaiming before him: 'Thus shall it be done to the man whom the king delights to honor.'"* The proclamation itself speaks to his ego. As if wearing the king's clothes and riding the king's horse is not sufficient, Haman has to make certain everyone knows the king himself delights to honor him.

Berlin summarizes Haman's advice to Ahasuerus very well:

> All of these details hint that Haman is aiming to take the place of the king. ... In fact, the root *m-l-k*, "king, royal" occurs seven times in Haman's speech in verses 8–9, suggesting that the kingship is surely on Haman's mind. He has already been designated as a person to whom everyone must bow, making him a kind of surrogate king, and now he wants to masquerade as the king, wearing the king's own robe and sitting on the king's own horse. All that

---

[84] Duguid, *Esther and Ruth*, 77. Ironically, the next line in Duguid's commentary is the title of the following section: "Haman's Terrible, Horrible, No Good, Very Bad Day."

[85] Reid, *Esther*, 120.

is missing is his taking the king's wife, and that is what it looks to Ahasuerus that he is doing in 7.8.[86]

### 4. A Patriot is Honored and an Egomaniac is Disgraced (6.10–11) [87]

Having created, in his mind, the perfect award ceremony for himself, Haman learns his arch-nemesis is to be honored in this way. It is striking that the two things Haman hates most about Mordecai—that he is a Jew and that he sits at the gate (cf. 5.13)—are used as the key identifying marks.[88]

Further, Haman's suggestion that "one of the king's most noble officials" (v 9) be the one to perform the honor backfires as Haman himself is in charge of honoring Mordecai. Laniak says,

> He had come to the palace this morning to seek the removal of Mordecai from his position of honor in the court only to be placed in charge of enhancing Mordecai's honor throughout the capital! With words that have the effect of 'rubbing it in,' the king reminds him to 'do just as *you* have suggested. ... Do not neglect anything *you* have recommended' (v 10). Haman unwittingly continues to design his own demise.[89]

**6.10,** *Then the king said to Haman,* The king is unaware of their mutual antagonism, which itself might be a meaningful coincidence of the chapter.[90] It certainly fits the satire of the king's never knowing what is going on in his own city. Baldwin says, "In his isolation he had no means of knowing what was evident to a child playing at the gate of his palace, but citizens

---

[86] Berlin, *Esther,* 60–61.

[87] Levenson, *Esther,* 93 uses this title for the entirety of chapter 6.

[88] Laniak, "Esther," 239.

[89] Ibid.

[90] Clines, *Ezra, Nehemiah, Esther,* 309.

who watched the parade through the city square could appreciate the irony and marvel at the incongruity." [91] Since no reactions of any kind—neither the participants nor the witnesses—are recorded, the reader is left to imagine what everyone must have been thinking.

*"Hurry; take the robes and the horse, as you have said, and do so to Mordecai the Jew, who sits at the king's gate."* As Bush says, "Haman's words are barely out of his mouth when the honor that he had so confidently envisioned as his own is transformed in an instant into abject and utter humiliation by one sentence from the king." [92] Firth points out that Mordecai's name is withheld until the very last moment, allowing Haman's ego to continue to swell until it was suddenly burst. [93] As Haman entered the palace, Mordecai's end was, "in his mind, tantalizingly close." [94] Instead, he is forced to honor Mordecai before all of the most important men of Susa.

Other than Haman's shock to learn it was for Mordecai, the king's answer is not surprising; he has not said "no" to any request he had heard yet. As Beal says, "Although Haman's proposal is outrageous, and although granting it should be out of the question for any self-respecting royal, we fully expect that the king will approve it, and so he does. The king follows Haman's recommendation without qualification." [95]

There is no contradiction between the edict to exterminate the Jews and Ahasuerus' desire to honor Mordecai the Jew. Nei-

---

[91] Baldwin, *Esther,* 90.

[92] Bush, *Ruth, Esther,* 420.

[93] Firth, *The Message of Esther,* 97.

[94] Phillips, "Esther," 646.

[95] Beal, "Esther," 83.

ther is it as confusing a matter as many commentators seem to suppose it is[96] for there is no reason to suppose Ahasuerus has been told the identity of the group Haman wished to kill, which he had intentionally not revealed in Esther 3. This may be surprising since everyone else in the city knows the ethnicity of the group in question but, as Bush says, is quite in keeping with the satirical way the narrator has characterized Ahasuerus.[97] On top of this, in the next chapter, Ahasuerus does not seem to remember the edict at all (7.5). His memory is short, as is already made evident by his failure to remember Mordecai's service.[98] Further, Mordecai represents no threat to the king's glory, so he is not at all reluctant to take Haman's advice—though one may wonder if he would have responded so positively if Haman had been the honoree.[99] Nor should there be any concern as to how Ahasuerus learned the ethnicity of Mordecai. Although the text does not say he was identified as such in the chronicles (cf. 2.19–23), neither does it say that it was kept hidden from the king.[100] Further, the use of "the Jew" here is titular, suggesting he was commonly called this to "distinguish him from others with the same theophorous name."[101] If so, the official record

---

[96] E.g., Huey, "Esther," 823: "It seems strange that the king would knowingly honor a Jew so soon after enacting an edict to destroy all the Jews in his kingdom." Cf. Moore, *Esther*, 65, who asks, "Would the king now exclude Mordecai from the pogrom? Would the king be more favorably disposed toward the Jews now that he knew Mordecai was Jewish?"

[97] Bush, *Ruth, Esther*, 416.

[98] Fox, *Character and Ideology*, 77.

[99] Reid, *Esther*, 120.

[100] Bush, *Ruth, Esther*, 416. Bush sets this in contrast with Esther's Jewishness and Esther's relationship to Mordecai, which the narrative makes clear is kept from Ahasuerus.

[101] Moore, *Esther*, 65. See Richard Bauckham, *Jesus and the Eyewitnesses* (Grand Rap-

may have included this disambiguation whether or not Esther 2 records it in this way. Even if it were not so recorded, the servants who read the record to Mordecai could have certainly provided the particulars to the king, since Mordecai frequented the king's gate.[102]

*"Leave out nothing that you have mentioned."* Haman is first shocked to hear the name Mordecai as the object of the honoring. Second, the knife is twisted as he is identified by the two things Haman hated most about him. Third, Ahasuerus emphasizes he is not to leave any of the honors out, so there can be no shortcuts. Finally, the king twice reminds Haman these are his own words, his instructions, rather than the king's.[103]

**6.11,** *So Haman took the robes and the horse, and he dressed Mordecai and led him through the square of the city, proclaiming before him, "Thus shall it be done to the man whom the king delights to honor."* The reversal begins. Mordecai is clothed in royalty, which Haman had coveted for himself, and Haman will soon adopt Mordecai's garments of mourning.[104] Further, as Haman must repeat concerning Mordecai the very statement he had taken such delight in as he imagined it applied to himself, the reader is reminded that, as before, Mordecai remains Haman's primary obstacle to the attainment of the honor he so desperately desired.[105]

The reactions of neither Haman nor Mordecai are included, perhaps because the reversal is more important to the narrative

---

ids: Eerdmans, 2006), 78–84 for a discussion of such ways of distinguishing people with common names in first century Jewish Palestine.

[102] Keil, "Esther," 226.

[103] Tomasino, *Esther, ad loc.*

[104] Clines, *Ezra, Nehemiah, Esther,* 309.

[105] Beal, "Esther," 84–85.

than their psychological or emotional state. Fox, however, argues that the silence itself speaks, "leaving the impression that nothing was said. Haman gritted his teeth and did what he had to do, while Mordecai taciturnly accepted the honor." [106] The silence, however, was not complete: Haman broke it repeatedly "by the intoning of the phrase that Haman so relished when he thought it was meant for him," [107] as "the thing that Mordecai would not do for Haman—bow down—Haman had to tell others to do for Mordecai." [108] Mordecai, unaware of what led to this sudden public honoring, may have felt it to be a cruel irony, since his people were destined for destruction and may have seen it as a scene of mockery rather than true honoring.[109]

### 5. *Fools Suddenly Wise* (6.12–13)

Haman returns to the scene of his previous pity party, only to find those who had earlier advised him to kill Mordecai have now changed their tunes rather significantly. Where was all of this insight earlier? Why have they had such a change of heart? Were there reservations all along, which they neglected to mention, or was Haman's humiliation enough to make them read the situation differently? Whatever the case may be, those who

---

[106] Fox, *Character and Ideology*, 78. Phillips, "Esther," 646 suggests the brief reporting may indicate Haman does his duty "as quickly and perfunctorily as possible." The Rabbis add a fanciful (but fantastic) embellishment. According to Cohen, *Megilath Esther*, 23, "When they passed by Haman's house, his daughter was watching from the roof. She thought that surely the one on the horse was her father, and the one leading it was Mordecai. She, therefore, seized the opportunity to throw the chamber pot on the one she thought to be Mordecai. When her father looked up, she recognized him and, in anguish, sprang from the roof, killing herself."

[107] Bush, *Ruth, Esther,* 420.

[108] Mangano, *Esther and Daniel,* 92.

[109] Phillips, "Esther," 646.

were previously only too happy to urge Haman on now seem only too anxious to abandon ship.[110]

**6.12,** *Then Mordecai returned to the king's gate.* Wells points out that the garments of celebration worn by Mordecai are superficial (as was the ceremony itself) because of the decree that was still in force: "[D]espite the satisfaction and *Schadenfreude* of Haman's humiliation, Mordecai is still facing impending death."[111] So, Mordecai returns to his normal station to do his normal work.

*But Haman hurried to his house…* The juxtaposition of verbs and destinations—Mordecai's return to the gate and Haman's hurrying to his house—is part of the larger contrast of Mordecai's public honoring and Haman's public shame. Haman's return home is also different from Mordecai, whose home we know nothing about. The narrative says very little as to the private life or inner psyche of Mordecai, which is set in stark contrast with the many windows into Haman's heart and home: "Unlike the typical villain of modern narrative, who is represented as having neither heart nor home, Esther's villain is perpetually exposed."[112]

*mourning and with his head covered.* Clothing is a significant motif in the Esther narrative and is here a clue to the change that is coming about. The Jews, upon learning of the edict, were covered with sackcloth and dust, as were Mordecai and Esther.

---

[110] Goldman, *The Five Megilloth,* The Soncino Books of the Bible (London: The Soncino Press, 1952), 226 suggests they may be referred to as "wise men" in an ironic sense since they are wise *after the fact.* Phillips, "Esther," 647 notes the shift from "friends" to "wise men" creates distance between them and Haman.

[111] Wells, "Esther," 66.

[112] Beal, "Esther," 85. See Fox, *Character and Ideology,* 178–179, 191–195 for character studies on Mordecai and Haman elaborating on Haman's transparency and Mordecai's reserve.

As Laniak says, "The first hint of the story's great reversal is Esther's act of clothing herself with royalty in 5.1. Haman is now covered with shame and Mordecai is clothed with the garments of royal honor. The shifting currents are hard to miss." [113] Rabanus Maurus sees God's working in this: "This is the change caused by the right hand of the Highest: the one who had just boasted about his power and was arrogant towards everyone else becomes viler and weaker than anyone else." [114]

In other Old Testament passages, covering one's head is a sign of mourning for the dead. [115] Fox says, "While the signs of mourning do not necessarily indicate mourning for the dead, they do mark the sorts of emotions associated with the situation. Haman is bewailing the death of his honor." [116]

**6.13,** *And Haman told his wife Zeresh and all his friends everything that had happened to him.* Humiliated, Haman returns to the advisers who had previously given him such splendid advice. Then, they offered counsel that was able to remove Haman's rage and frustration concerning Mordecai, and he surely hopes for a similar solution to his current problem of shame. [117]

*Then his wise men and his wife Zeresh said to him, "If Mordecai, before whom you have begun to fall, is of the Jewish people, you will not overcome him but will surely fall before him."* Berlin points to

---

[113] Laniak, "Esther," 240.

[114] Conti, *1–2 Kings, 1–2 Chronicles, Ezra, Nehemiah, Esther,* 389.

[115] Bush, *Ruth, Esther,* 416. Tomasino, *Esther, ad loc.* suggests another, more practical reason to cover his head: trying to avoid being seen and mocked by all of the officials who knew Mordecai was Haman's dread enemy.

[116] Fox, *Character and Ideology,* 79.

[117] Beal, "Esther," 86.

another reversal here: just as in Esther 3, Mordecai's fate became the fate of his people, so once again it is.[118]

Nearly every commentator points out that the conditional clause is not truly conditional here but causal since Zeresh knew of Mordecai's ethnicity (cf. 5.13). Many commentators suggest Zeresh is speaking for the narrator's convictions at this point. Clines, for example, says, "[C]ould his counsellors be voicing the narrator's belief in the predictions of the fall of Amalek before Israel (Exod 17.16; Num 24.20; 1 Sam 15.2f; cf. 2 Sam 1.8f, 13–16)? If so, they speak on behalf not only of the narrator but of diaspora Jewry generally."[119] Firth adds, "What Persians might see only as an unexplainable element about Jewish survival is in reality a truth that is grounded in Scripture, and beyond that in the faithfulness of God."[120]

It is striking that we are told how the first advice given to Haman pleased him, but no comment is made about his reaction to this word; presumably, he was much less pleased.[121] The lack of time for him even to react before being swept off to the feast (where the reader knows his demise awaits) may be part of the rhetorical effect of the situation spiraling out of his control.

### 6. *Haman's Hasty Departure* (6.14)

This verse marks the transition from the scene at Haman's house to the second banquet.[122] In so doing, it continues the fast pace

---

[118] Berlin, *Esther*, 63.

[119] Clines, *Ezra, Nehemiah, Esther*, 310. Cf. Roop, *Ruth, Jonah, Esther*, 222.

[120] Firth, *The Message of Esther*, 98.

[121] Roop, *Ruth, Jonah, Esther*, 221.

[122] Commentators differ on whether to include this verse with chapter 6 or 7. Bush, *Ruth, Esther*, 412–413 makes a compelling case to see 5.9–6.14 as a single unit based on a series of inclusios that tie them together, though it is also clearly transitional to chapter 7.

of motion that has characterized the end of Esther 6 as Haman feels his life spinning out of control. Now, instead of being able to go joyfully to the feast at his leisure as he planned (5.14), he is hurried off by the king's eunuchs.

**6.14,** *While they were yet talking with him, the king's eunuchs arrived and hurried to bring Haman to the feast that Esther had prepared.* The conversation is not even complete when his escorts arrive to rush him away—taken from a scene of utter humiliation to the scene of his own execution.[123] There is no time to recover from the first incident before the second begins. The rush "keeps Haman moving swiftly and inexorably to his doom."[124] Suddenly, for the first time, Haman has no control. Fox points out the significance of the sudden passivity: "Haman, the skilled manipulator of the king's will and (he hopes) a people's destiny, is no longer in control of his own life. He is rushed out and taken to a situation that *Esther* has prepared. He has been brought to *her* territory, and the initiative is now with her."[125]

---

[123] Roop, *Ruth, Jonah, Esther,* 219, says, "Haman *hurried* home (6.12) but does not even have opportunity to conclude his conversation with his wife before the story itself hurries on (6.14). From this moment, the story moves quickly to the decisive scene, the downfall of Haman."

[124] Berlin, *Esther,* 64.

[125] Fox, *Character and Ideology,* 81. Haman's passivity and Esther's initiative is especially interesting in light of Esther's character development. See chapter 8, above.

## B. Conclusion

Esther 6 is distinctly the center point of the Esther narrative, as can be seen from two different perspectives. First, the narrative itself has a chiastic structure, and Esther 6 is the center of the chiasm. Second, a series of ironic reversals make up the narrative framework of Esther, which exhibit the same inverse parallelism as the structure itself. Esther 6 is the pivot on which the fortunes of Haman turn and the reversals begin. This central chapter and point at which the narrative turns does not feature either of the human heroes of Esther but only a series of unlikely coincidences. In fact, by the time Esther returns to the narrative, a positive outcome for the Jews is already visible.[126] Beal summarizes the reversals very well: "According to Haman's plan (5.14), by this point Mordecai should be hanging on a fifty-foot stake in ultimate shame, and he should be happily on his way to Esther's second drinking party. Instead his mind is filled with echoes of the dooming words of his wife and friends, and with a dreadful vision of Mordecai looking more like the king than the king himself does."[127]

Fox offers a helpful summary of Esther 6 that captures much of what has been said above:

> [This scene] is without practical effect on the progress of events. Haman remains vizier and Mordecai returns to the gate. The significance of this episode is structural: it holds the book's turning point and sets Haman on his way to destruction. Haman, as his associates recognize, has now *begun* to fall. He is deprived of the royal insignia he had hoped for, and they are given to Mordecai instead. This foreshadows the transfer of vizerial power. ... The

---

[126] Reid, *Esther*, 121.

[127] Beal, "Esther," 86.

forward momentum of Haman's scheme has been broken. He is
on the way down, Mordecai is on the way up.[128]

But is it merely coincidence that brings about the reversals,
the positive outcome, the humiliation of Haman, and the honoring of Mordecai? Given the author's theological framing of
the book, as discussed earlier, Esther 6 points us squarely in the
direction of God's providence. Inasmuch as the book of Esther
is framed in a religious context, it has religious implications.

---

[128] Fox, *Character and Ideology*, 82.

# Recommended Reading for Further Study

Since I began serious study of Esther, I have frequently been asked for commentary recommendations by those who are approaching this book for the first time. In an effort to expand previous thoughts offered to various individuals and compile my thinking on these matters in a single place, I've included this appendix. I fully realize that it will not be helpful to everyone and that there is certainly room for debate in my evaluation. Nor is it exhaustive, even if it seems that way to someone new to Esther research.[129]

## Commentaries

My recommendation for Esther commentaries usually begins with **Laniak** (Understanding the Bible Commentary [formerly NIBC], bound with Allen on Ezra-Nehemiah). Among the four or five commentaries I first read, this was the most formative for my thinking. Laniak wrote his Harvard Divinity dissertation on Esther under Jon Levenson, so even though there are series-related constraints on the depth and length, sound scholarship backs up every word. His writing is clear and easy to comprehend and the series' constraints help make this volume accessible to anyone.

---

[129] This appendix was not included in the Advance Review Copy that was sent to various Esther scholars, including those who chose to endorse this book, so my comments on their works did not, *quid pro quo*, influence their comments on mine.

After Laniak comes **Bush** (Word Biblical Commentary, bound with Ruth) and **Levenson** (Old Testament Library). Bush is among the most exhaustive and technical commentaries on Esther, which makes it invaluable for digging into various perspectives on the text. Levenson provides excellent insights throughout and includes commentary on the LXX additions, which most commentaries omit.

Less technical, but worth the investment of time are **Jobes** (NIV Application Commentary), **Clines** (New Century Biblical Commentary, bound with Ezra and Nehemiah), and **Berlin** (JPS Bible Commentary). Because of the nature of the NIVAC—requiring a practical application for every pericope—the series can be inconsistent even within a single volume. Overall, Jobes does a good job with the text and thinking through some of those issues. I have heard several call Jobes' volume their favorite Esther commentary, so she has clearly written a work that resonates. Clines is a top-flight Old Testament scholar and, in this volume, you get what you would expect: very good exegesis within the framework of the set's limitations. Berlin, a Jewish exegete, is insightful in a variety of ways, but particularly if the reader has never considered Old Testament texts from a modern, Jewish perspective.

Shorter, more accessible, but very helpful commentaries are **Baldwin** (Tyndale Old Testament Commentaries), **Reid** (Tyndale replacement volume), and **Firth** (The Bible Speaks Today). For those familiar with these series, there will not be much surprise: solid, conservative exegetes providing solid exposition. Those who want more than a popular exposition can offer but are not ready to tackle more scholarly writing would do well with any of these—though I will say that I believe Reid's replacement has surpassed Baldwin, in spite of my great respect for the latter. Firth is solid throughout and would also be an excellent choice from this group.

On a similar level are **Huey** (Expositor's Bible Commentary, bound with various authors on Kings–Job), **Phillips** (Expositor's replacement volume, bound with various authors on Chronicles–Job; both Expositor's volumes contain Yamauchi on Ezra and Nehemiah, which adds to the value of either book), and **Breneman** (New American Commentary, bound with Ezra and Nehemiah). Of the two Expositor's volumes, Phillips is definitely the one to read. Breneman is fine, but did not add much that others did not already say.

A few popular-level commentaries are worth reading. Best among these expositions is undoubtedly **Duguid** (Reformed Expositor's Commentary, bound with Ruth), who is, as usual, fantastic. The nature of the series prevents it from being academic, but Duguid is an outstanding writer and provides an excellent exposition, especially given the restraints of the series. **McConville** (Daily Study Bible) is given very little space, but squeezes the most out of it that he can. The reader will not find incredible depth here, but there are insights worth seeking.

Most popular-level commentaries, however, are minimally helpful, at best. Among those worth mentioning are **Whitcomb** (Everyman's Bible Commentary), who asserts a hardline conservative perspective at every point without much argument; in fairness, this may be due to the nature and constraints of the series. **Bechtel** (Interpretation) typically has more helpful information, but still lacks the depth to be of much use to most students. **Roop** (Believers Church Bible Commentary, bound with Ruth and Jonah) is a good thinker, but is thin on Esther.

More difficult to sift through are the works of **Paton** (International Critical Commentary), **Keil** (Keil and Delitzsch Commentary on the Old Testament, bound with Ezra–Job), and **Moore** (Anchor Bible). The most interesting feature of Paton is some unique information that he provides in his introduction and the historical significance of the volume in Esther's history of interpretation. Keil is dated and can be difficult to read, but can also provide excellent insight for the student willing to work through it. Moore is, in my view, hit or miss; the introduction may be the best part of the volume.

A few unique commentaries that are worth mentioning begin with **Beal** (Berit Olam Studies in Hebrew Narrative and Poetry, bound with Linafelt on Ruth). While he engages in commentary on the verses, he is more interested literary analysis. The reader may not agree with his every conclusion, but the unique approach is worth considering. Less detailed is **Murphy** (Forms of Old Testament Literature, bound with the Wisdom Literature), a form-critical commentary that examines matters such as structure, genre, setting, and intent. **Wells** (Brazos Theological Commentary on the Bible, bound with Sumner on Daniel) approaches the text through a theological and doctrinal lens, rather than strict exegesis. Different still is **Conti** (Ancient Christian Commentary), a compilation of quotes from the church fathers.

Two final commentaries that I have limited interaction with are **Tomasino** (Evangelical Exegetical Commentary) and **Mangano** (College Press NIV Commentary). Of the two, Tomasino is the most scholarly and exhaustive, though I have found helpful insights in both.

Forthcoming commentaries that I am aware of include **Hubbard** (New International Commentary on the Old Testament), **Rogland** (Zondervan Exegetical Commentary on the Old Testament), **Klingbeil** (Apollos Old Testament Commentary), **Taylor** (Story of God Bible Commentary), **Schmutzer** (Teach the Text), **Hill** (Biblical Theology for Christian Proclamation), and **Hogg** (Reformation Commentary on Scripture, bound with Ezra and Nehemiah).

## Other Works

In addition to the commentaries, many other helpful works on Esther have been written. **Fox's** *Character and Ideology in the Book of Esther* is probably the top of this group. Fox provides detailed character analysis as well as a brief commentary on the whole book. Nearly every expositor since its writing has been influenced by it to some degree and no serious study of the book should be attempted without consulting this volume.

More recently is **Dunne's** *Esther and Her Elusive God.* Dunne has written a very accessible volume focused on the question of religion in the book of Esther that has the potential to be extremely influential as well. The reader may not agree with Dunne's every conclusion, but everyone should at least wrestle with the issues he raises.

A work that is not specifically on Esther but bears mentioning is **Webb's** *Five Festal Garments* (New Studies in Biblical Theology), a collection of essays on the five megilloth. Each essay is roughly 20 pages and, though it does not have space to cover much in depth, provides excellent insight into the books without being merely "introductory."

The last group of books are mostly for specialists looking to exhaust every corner of Esther study. They tend to be very specific in their focus. They include **Laniak's** *Shame and Honor in the Book of Esther* (SBL Dissertation Series), **Jobes'** *The Alpha-Text of Esther* (SBL Dissertation Series), **Clines'** *Esther Scroll: The Story of the Story* (JSOT Supplement Series) and **Fox's** *The Redaction of the Books of Esther* (SBL Monograph Series).

# Bibliography

Alexander, T.D. "Jonah: An Introduction and Commentary." *Obadiah, Jonah, Micah.* Tyndale Old Testament Commentaries. Downers Grove: Inter-Varsity Press, 1988.

Alter, R. *The Art of Biblical Narrative.* New York: Basic Books, 1981.

Anderson, B.W. "The Place of the Book of Esther in the Christian Bible." *Journal of Religion* 30 (1950): 32–43.

Archer, G.L. *A Survey of Old Testament Introduction.* Chicago: Moody Press, 1974.

Baldwin, J.G. *Esther: An Introduction and Commentary.* Tyndale Old Testament Commentaries. Downers Grove, Inter-Varsity Press, 1984.

———. *1 and 2 Samuel: An Introduction and Commentary.* Tyndale Old Testament Commentaries. Downers Grove: IVP Academic, 1988.

———. *Daniel: An Introduction and Commentary.* Tyndale Old Testament Commentaries. Downers Grove: Intervarsity Press, 1978.

Barclay, J.M.G. *Jews in the Mediterranean Diaspora: From Alexander to Trajan (323 BCE–117 CE).* Oakland: University of California Press, 1999.

Bar-Efrat, S. "Some Observations on the Analysis of Structure in Biblical Narrative." *Vetus Testamentum* 30 (1980): 1972.

Bauckham, Richard. *Jesus and the Eyewitnesses: The Gospels as Eyewitness Testimony.* Grand Rapids: Eerdmans, 2006.

Beal, T.K. "Esther." *Berit Olam: Ruth and Esther.* Collegeville: The Liturgical Press, 1999.

Beckett, M. *Gospel in Esther.* Carlisle: Paternoster Press, 2002.

Bechtel, C. *Esther.* Interpretation. Louisville: John Knox Press, 2002.

Beckwith, R.T. *The Old Testament Canon of the New Testament Church and its Background in Early Judaism.* London: SPCK, 1985.

Beller, D. "A Theology of the Book of Esther." *Restoration Quarterly* 39 no. 1 (1997): 1–15.

Berg, S. *The Book of Esther: Motifs, Themes and Structure.* SBL Dissertation Series 44. Missoula: Scholars Press, 1979.

Berlin, A. *Esther.* The JPS Bible Commentary. Philadelphia: The Jewish Publication Society, 2001.

_____. "The Book of Esther and Ancient Storytelling." *Journal of Biblical Literature* 120 no. 1 (2001): 3–14.

Birch, B.C., et al. *A Theological Introduction to the Old Testament.* 2nd ed. Nashville: Abingdon Press, 2005.

Bland, D. "God's Activity as Reflected in the Books of Ruth and Esther." *Restoration Quarterly* 24 no. 3 (1981): 129–147.

Blomberg, C.L.. *1 Corinthians.* The NIV Application Commentaray. Grand Rapids: Zondervan, 1994.

Breneman, M. *Ezra-Nehemiah, Esther.* New American Commentary. Nashville: Broadman & Holman Publishers, 1993.

Brighton, L.A. "The Book of Esther: Textual and Canonical Considerations." *Concordia Journal* 13 no. 3 (Jl 1987): 200–218.

Bush, F.W. *Ruth/Esther.* Word Biblical Commentary. Nashville: Nelson Reference & Electronic, 1996.

_____. "The Book of Esther: *Opus non gratum* in the Christian Canon." *Bulletin for Biblical Research* 8 (1998): 39-54.

Clines, D.J.A. *Ezra, Nehemiah, Esther.* The New Century Bible Commentary. Grand Rapids: Eerdmans, 1984.

_____. "In Quest of the Historical Mordecai." *Vetus Testamentum* 41 no. 2 (1991): 129–136.

_____. *The Esther Scroll: The Story of the Story.* Journal for the Study of the Old Testament Supplement Series 30. Sheffield: JSOT, 1984.

Collins, J.J. *Between Athens and Jerusalem: Jewish Identity in the Hellenistic Diaspora,* 2nd ed. Grand Rapids: Eerdmans, 2000.

Collins, N.L. "Did Esther Fast on the 15th Nisan? An Extended Comment on Esther 3.12." *Revue Biblique* 100 (1993): 533–561.

Cohen, A. and A J. Rosenberg, eds. *Megillath Esther: Hebrew Text and English Translation with an Introduction and Commentary.* Rev. ed. London: Soncino Press, 1984.

Conti, M. *1–2 Kings, 1–2 Chronicles, Ezra, Nehemiah, Esther.* Ancient Christian Commentary on Scripture. Downers Grove: Inter-Varsity Press, 2008.

Cornhill, C.H. *Einleitung in das Alte Testament.* Leipzig: 1891.

deSilva, D.A. *Introducing the Apocrypha: Message, Context, and Significance.* Grand Rapids: Baker Academic, 2002.

Dillard, R.B. and T. Longman III. *An Introduction to the Old Testament.* Grand Rapids: Zondervan, 1994.

Dorsey, D. *The Literary Structure of the Old Testament: A Commentary on Genesis–Malachi*. Grand Rapids: Baker Books, 1999.

Duguid, I. *Esther and Ruth*. Reformed Expository Commentary. Phillipsburg: P&R Publishing, 2005.

_____. "But Did They Live Happily Ever After? The Eschatology of the Book of Esther." *Westminster Theological Journal* 68 (2006): 85–98.

Dunne, J.A. *Esther and Her Elusive God: How a Secular Story Functions as Scripture*. Eugene: Wipf & Stock, 2014.

Eissfeldt, O. *The Old Testament: An Introduction*. New York: Harper and Row, 1965.

Fee, G.D. *The First Epistle to the Corinthians*. The New International Commentary on the New Testament. Grand Rapids: Eerdmans, 1987.

Ferguson, Everett. *Backgrounds of Early Christianity*, 3rd ed. Grand Rapids: Eerdmans, 2003.

Firth, D.G. "The Book of Esther: A Neglected Paradigm for Dealing with the State." *Old Testament Essays* 10, no. 1 (1997): 18–26.

_____. *The Message of Esther: God Present But Unseen*. The Bible Speaks Today. Downers Grove: Inter-Varsity Press, 2010.

_____. "The Third Quest for the Historical Mordecai and the Genre of the Book of Esther." *Old Testament Essays* 16, no. 2 (2003): 233–243.

_____. "When Samuel Met Esther: Narrative Focalism, Intertextuality, and Theology." *Southeastern Theological Review* 1 no. 1 (2010): 15–28.

Fox, M.V. *Character and Ideology in the Book of Esther.* 2nd ed. Grand Rapids: Eerdmans, 2001.

_____. *The Redaction of the Book of Esther: On Reading Composite Texts.* Society of Biblical Literature Monograph Series 40. Atlanta: Scholars Press, 1991.

_____. "The Religion of the Book of Esther." *Judaism* 39 no. 2 (Spr 1990): 135–147.

Garland, D.E. *1 Corinthians.* Baker Exegetical Commentary on the New Testament. Grand Rapids: Baker Academic, 2003.

_____. *Colossians and Philemon.* The NIV Application Commentary. Grand Rapids: Zondervan, 1998.

Goldman, S. "Narrative and Ethical Ironies in Esther." *Journal of the Study of the Old Testament* 47 (1990): 15–31.

_____. *The Five Megilloth,* 2nd ed. The Soncino Books of the Bible. London: The Soncino Press, 1952.

Gordis, R. "Religion, Wisdom and History in the Book of Esther—A New Solution to an Ancient Crux." *Journal of Biblical Literature* 100 no. 3 (1981): 359–388.

_____. "Studies in the Esther Narrative." *Journal of Biblical Literature* 95 no. 1 (1976): 43–58.

Goswell, G.R. "Keeping God out of the Book of Esther." *Evangelical Quarterly* 82 no. 2 (2010): 99–110.

Grossman, J. "'Dynamic Analogies' in the Book of Esther." *Vetus Testamentum* 59 (2009): 394–414.

Gruen, E.S. *Diaspora: Jews Amidst Greeks and Romans.* Cambridge: Harvard University Press, 2002.

Hamilton, T. "The Book of Joel." *Minor Prophets I: Hosea–Micah.* Truth Commentaries. Bowling Green: Guardian of Truth Foundation, 2007.

Hamilton, V. *Handbook on the Historical Books*. Grand Rapids: Baker Academic, 2001.

_____. *The Book of Genesis: Chapters 18–50*. The New International Commentary on the Old Testament. Grand Rapids: Eerdmans, 1995.

Harrison, R.K. *Introduction to the Old Testament*. 1969. Peabody: Prince Press, 1999.

Hays, J.D. *The Message of the Prophets: A Survey of the Prophetic and Apocalyptic Books of the Old Testament*. Grand Rapids: Zondervan, 2010.

Hoerth, A.J. *Archaeology and the Old Testament*. Grand Rapids: Baker Academic, 1998.

Horn, S.H. "Mordecai: A Historical Problem." *Biblical Research* 9 (1964): 14–25.

Howard, D. *An Introduction to the Old Testament Historical Books*. Chicago: Moody Press, 1993.

Hubbard, D.A. *Joel and Amos: An Introduction and Commentary*. Tyndale Old Testament Commentaries. Downers Grove: Inter-Varsity Press, 1989.

Huey, F.B. "Esther." *1 & 2 Kings, 1 & 2 Chronicles, Ezra, Nehemiah, Esther, Job*. The Expositor's Bible Commentary. Grand Rapids: Zondervan, 1988.

_____. "Irony as the Key to Understanding the Book of Esther." *Southwestern Journal of Theology* 32 no. 3 (Sum 1990): 36–39.

Humphreys, W.L. "A Life-Style for Diaspora: A Study of the Tales of Esther and Daniel." *Journal of Biblical Literature* 92 no. 2 (1973): 211–223.

Jackowski, K. "Holy Disobedience in Esther." *Theology Today* 45 no. 4 (1989): 403–414.

Jobes, K. *Esther.* The NIV Application Commentary. Grand Rapids: Zondervan, 1999.

_____. *The Alpha-Text of Esther: Its Character and Relationship to the Masoretic Text.* Society of Biblical Literature Dissertation Series 153. Atlanta: Scholars Press, 1996.

_____ and M. Silva. *Invitation to the Septuagint.* Grand Rapids: Baker Academic, 2000.

Jones, B.W. "Two Misconceptions about the Book of Esther." *Catholic Biblical Quarterly* 39 no. 2 (1977): 171–181.

Keil, C.F. "Esther." *Ezra, Nehemiah, Esther, Job.* Commentary on the Old Testament. Peabody: Hendrickson Publishers, 2001.

Kidner, D. *Genesis: An Introduction and Commentary.* Tyndale Old Testament Commentaries. Downers Grove: Inter-Varsity Press, 1967.

Kitchen, K.A. *On the Reliability of the Old Testament.* Grand Rapids: Eerdmans, 2003.

Klein, R.W. *Textual Criticism of the Old Testament: From the Septuagint to Qumran* Philadelphia: Fortress Press, 1974.

Laniak, T.K. "Esther." *Ezra, Nehemiah, Esther.* New International Biblical Commentary. Peabody: Hendrickson, 2003.

_____. *Shame and Honor in the Book of Esther.* SBL Dissertation Series 165. Atlanta: Scholars Press, 1998.

Lehman, M. "The Literary Study of Esther." *Biblical Viewpoint* 26 (1992): 85–95.

Lerner, B.D. "No Happy Ending for Esther." *Jewish Bible Quarterly* 29, no 1 (2001): 4–12.

Levenson, J.D. *Esther: A Commentary.* Old Testament Library. Louisville: John Knox Press, 1997.

Lightfoot, N.R. *How We Got the Bible.* Grand Rapids: Baker Books, 2003.

Loader, J.A. "Esther as a Novel with Different Levels of Meaning." *Zeitschrift für die alttestamentliche Wissenchaft* 90 no 3 (1978): 417–421.

Mangano, M. *Esther & Daniel.* The College Press NIV Commentary. Joplin: College Press, 2001.

McClarty, W. "Esther." *A Complete Literary Guide to the Bible.* Grand Rapids: Zondervan, 1993.

McConville, J.G. *Ezra, Nehemiah, and Esther.* The Daily Study Bible Series. Philadelphia: The Westminster Press, 1985.

McGarvey, J.W. "Divine Providence: Queen Esther." *McGarvey's Sermons: Delivered in Louisville, Kentucky, June–September, 1893.* Delight: Gospel Light Publishing Company, n.d.

McGee, J.V. *Ezra, Nehemiah, and Esther.* Thru the Bible Commentary Series. Nashville: Thomas Nelson, 1991.

McGeough, K. "Esther the Hero: Going beyond 'Wisdom' in Heroic Narratives." *Catholic Biblical Quarterly* 70 no. 1 (Ja 2008): 44–65.

McGuiggan, J. *Celebrating the Wrath of God: Reflections on the Agony and Ecstasy of His Relentless Love.* Colorado Springs: Waterbrook Press, 2001.

Millard, A.R. "The Persian Names in Esther and the Reliability of the Hebrew Text." *Journal of Biblical Literature* 96 (1977): 481–48.

Moo, Douglas J. *The Letters to the Colossians and to Philemon.* The Pillar New Testament Commentary. Grand Rapids: Eerdmans, 2008.

Moore, C.A. "Archaeology and the Book of Esther." *The Biblical Archaeologist* 38 (1975): 62–79.

_____. *Daniel, Esther, and Jeremiah: The Additions: A New Translation with Introduction and Commentary.* The Anchor Bible. Garden City: Doubleday & Company, 1977.

_____. "Eight Questions Most Frequently Asked about the Book of Esther." *Bible Review* 3 (1987): 16–31.

_____. *Esther: A New Translation with Introduction and Commentary.* The Anchor Bible. Garden City: Doubleday & Company, 1971.

_____. "On the Origins of the LXX Additions to the Book of Esther." *Journal of Biblical Literature* 92 (1973): 382–393.

Morris, A.E. "The Purpose of the Book of Esther." *Expository Times* 42 (1930–1931): 124–128.

Murphy, R.E. "Esther." *Wisdom Literature: Job, Proverbs, Ruth, Canticles, Ecclesiastes, and Esther.* The Forms of Old Testament Literature. Grand Rapids: Eerdmans, 1981.

Partlow, J.A. "Tough Decisions in the Silence of God: Esther 4.13–14." *Restoration Quarterly* 35 no. 4 (1993): 240–244.

Paton, L.B. *A Critical and Exegetical Commentary on The Book of Esther.* The International Critical Commentary. Edinburgh: T. & T. Clark, 1908.

Pfeiffer, R. *Introduction to the Old Testament* New York: Harper & Brothers, 1948.

Pfeiffer, R. H. *History of New Testament Times, with an Introduction to the Apocrypha.* New York: Harper & Brothers, 1949.

Phillips, E. "Esther." *1 Chronicles–Job.* The Expositor's Bible Commentary. Grand Rapids: Zondervan, 2010.

Pickup, M. "Canonicity of the Bible." *Reemphasizing Bible Basics.* Florida College Annual Lectures. Temple Terrace: Florida College Bookstore, 1990.

_____. "New Testament Interpretation of the Old Testament: The Theological Rationale of Midrashic Exegesis." *Journal of the Evangelical Theological Society* 51 no. 2 (2008): 353–381.

Pierce, R.W. "The Politics of Esther and Mordecai." *Bulletin for Biblical Research* 2 (1992): 75–89.

Provan, I., et al. *A Biblical History of Israel.* Louisville: Westminster John Knox Press, 2003.

Reid, D. *Esther: An Introduction and Commentary.* Tyndale Old Testament Commentaries. Downers Grove: Inter-Varsity Press, 2008.

Roberts, M. *Ezra, Nehemiah, Esther.* The Preacher's Commentary. Nashville: Thomas Nelson, 1993.

Roop, E.F. *Ruth, Jonah, Esther.* Believers Church Bible Commentary. Scottdale: Herald Press, 2002.

Rosenheim, J. "Fate and Freedom in the Scroll of Esther." *Prooftexts* 12 (1992): 125–149.

Rossow, F.C. "Literary Artistry in the Book of Esther and Its Theological Significance." *Concordia Journal* 13 no. 3 (Jl 1987): 219–233.

Sandmel, S. *The Enjoyment of Scripture.* New York: Oxford, 1972.

Sasson, J.M. "Esther." *The Literary Guide to the Bible.* Edited by Robert Alter and Frank Kermode. Cambridge: Belknap Press, 1987.

Segal, E. "Human Anger and Divine Intervention in Esther." *Prooftexts* 9 (1989): 247–256.

Shea, W.H. "Esther and History." *Concordia Journal* 13 no. 3 (Jl 1987): 234–248.

Stern, E.R. "Esther and the Politics of Diaspora." *The Jewish Quarterly Review* 100 no. 1 (2010): 99–110).

Stuart D., *Hosea–Jonah.* Word Biblical Commentaries. Nashville: Thomas Nelson, 1987.

Swindoll, C.R. *Esther: A Woman of Strength and Dignity.* Nashville: Word Publishing, 1997.

Talmon, S. "'Wisdom' in the Book of Esther." *Vetus Testamentum* 13 no. 4 (1963): 419–455.

Teuffel, J. "Fate and Word: The Book of Esther as Guidance to a Canonical Reading of Scripture." *Currents in Theology and Mission* 36 (2009): 26–31.

Thornton, T.C.G. "The Crucifixion of Haman and the Scandal of the Cross." *Journal of Theological Studies* 37 (1986): 419–426.

Tomasino, A. *Esther.* Evangelical Exegetical Commentary. Bellingham: Lexham Press, 2003.

Ungand A. "Keilinschriftliche Beiträge zum Buch Ezra und Esther." *Zeitschrift für die alttestamentliche Wissenschaft* 58 (1940–1941): 240–244.

Walfish, B.D. "Kosher Adultery: The Mordecai-Esther-Ahasuerus Triangle in Midrash and Exegesis." *Prooftexts* 22 (2002): 305–333.

Waltke, B.K. with C.J. Fredricks. *Genesis: A Commentary.* Grand Rapids: Zondervan, 2001.

Ward, K. "Seek the Welfare of the City." *Living in Captivity: God's People in a Time of Crisis.* Florida College Annual Lectures. Temple Terrace: FC Press, 2010

Ward, N. *The Growth of the Seed: Notes on the Book of Genesis.* Chillicothe: DeWard Publishing Co., 2007.

Watson, W.S. "The Authenticity and Genuineness of the Book of Esther." *The Princeton Theological Review* 1 (1903): 62–74.

Webb, B.G. *Five Festal Garments: Christian Reflections on the Song of Songs, Ruth, Lamentations, Ecclesiastes and Esther.* New Studies in Biblical Theology. Downers Grove: InterVarsity Press, 2000.

Weiland, F.S. "Historicity, Genre, and Narrative Design in the Book of Esther." *Bibliotheca Sacra* 159 (2002): 151–165.

_____. "Literary Clues to God's Providence in the Book of Esther." *Bibliotheca Sacra* 160 (2003): 37–47.

_____. "Literary Conventions in the Book of Esther." *Bibliotheca Sacra* 159 (2002): 425–435.

_____. "Plot Structure in the Book of Esther." *Bibliotheca Sacra* 159 (2002): 277–287.

Weisman, Z. *Political Satire in the Bible.* Atlanta: Scholars Press, 1998.

Wells, S. "Esther." *Esther & Daniel.* Brazos Theological Commentary on the Bible. Grand Rapids: Brazos Press, 2013.

Wechsler, M.G. "Shadow and Fulfillment in the Book of Esther." *Bibliotheca Sacra* 154 (1997): 275–284.

Wenham, G.J. *Genesis 16–50.* Word Biblical Commentary. Dallas: Word, 1994.

Whitcomb, J. *Esther: Triumph of God's Sovereignty.* Everyman's Bible Commentary. Chicago: Moody Press, 1979.

Wiebe, J.M. "Esther 4:14: 'Will Relief and Deliverance Arise for the Jews from Another Place?'" *Catholic Biblical Quarterly* 53 no. 3 (1991): 409–415.

Wood, L. *A Survey of Israel's History.* Grand Rapids: Zondervan, 1970.

Wright, J. S. "The Historicity of the Book of Esther." *New Perspectives on the Old Testament.* Waco: Word Books, 1970.

Yamauchi, E. "Mordecai, The Persepolis Tablets, and the Susa Excavations." *Vetus Testamentum* 42 no. 2 (1992):272–275.

_____. *Persia and the Bible.* Grand Rapids: Baker Book House, 1990.

_____. "The Archaeological Background of Esther." *Bibliotheca Sacra* 137 (1980): 99–117.

Young, E.J. *An Introduction to the Old Testament.* Grand Rapids: Zondervan, 1949.

Zadok, R. "On the Historical Background of the Book of Esther." *Biblische Notizen* 24 (1984): 18–23.

# Author Index

# Scripture Index

# Subject Index

# *Also By Nathan Ward*

## The Growth of the Seed
*Notes on the Book of Genesis*

A study of the book of Genesis that emphasizes two primary themes: the development
of the Messianic line and the growing enmity between the righteous and the wicked.
In addition, it provides detailed comments
on the text and short essays on several subjects that are suggested in, yet peripheral to,
Genesis. 537 pages. $19.99 (PB).

## Daybreak
*A Guide to Overcoming Temptation*

The sun rose on Jacob after his wrestling
match with God. A new day dawned and
he had a new name to match his new life. A
similar call for daybreak is made for Christians today: come out of the darkness and
into God's marvelous light (1 Pet 2.9). As
Christians, we must not live in the night.
We have experienced our own daybreak and
should walk in the light—but far too often,
we find the darkness alluring. *Daybreak* examines the call to overcome temptation, a
closer look at the enemy, and some practical
principles for winning the battle with sin. 108 pages. $8.99 (PB).

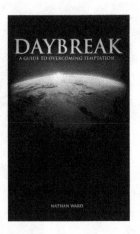

*For a full listing of DeWard Publishing Company books, visit our website:*

**www.deward.com**